D1825219

100 Steps

Happier

- From A Good Way To Think -

- Created by David Burvill -

www.AGoodWayToThink.com
Second Edition. First published 2016 All Rights Reserved. ISBN 978-1-326-65098-8
Text copyright © David Burvill. All rights reserved.
The moral right of the author has been asserted.

FOR YOU

BEFORE WE BEGIN...

There is a curiosity, somewhere underneath a veneer of scepticism, that can change the entire world. Like the sun on a cloudy day, the curiosity may sometimes be covered in doubt, scepticism, or complacency, but they keep on shining anyway. Curiosity is the light that keeps children giggling, keeps scientists questioning, and keeps the wise folk smiling. Opening up this book will feed that curiosity with the tools and exercises that can empower you to make your current life even happier.

By this point, the clouds and the doubts are probably very real! How can reading this optimistic little book possibly make you any happier than you already are? Well, it can't. Reading these pages in the hope they will make us happier is like shutting our eyes and trying to be taller. This is a guidebook full of actionable exercises, some of which were developed within the modern positive psychology movement tackling happiness with a scientific approach, others developed through centuries of Buddhist practice, and some exercises were developed by A Good Way To Think via the happiness training courses and coaching programs we run.

This guidebook follows a structured approach, dissecting the elements of our lives that impact our happiness, and explains tried and tested exercises that empower us to develop the specific skills and habits that influence how we experience happiness.

Practising these kinds of exercises has been repeatedly proven by peer-reviewed studies to have phenomenal positive effects on virtually every aspect of our lives; from physical and mental health to our work and relationships. Spending time prioritising happiness has been directly linked with increased life expectancy, boosted immune systems, lower rates of disease progression, and improved cognitive functioning, including better memory retention, better decision-making and increased creativity. When we take the time to better understand happiness and the mechanics of its influencing factors, we increase our emotional intelligence, meaning we can enjoy even more meaningful, nourishing relationships, while learning to experience more rewarding emotional responses too! We learn how to be even happier.

So, if it is this well established that the field of happiness is so beneficial to us, how can we positively influence it?

All good journeys start with a single step. You have picked up this book so we are already marching down this wonderful path. To keep heading in the best direction, there are a few things to aim for and a few things to avoid.

Complacency is the thickest barrier to our happiness, covering up curiosity like a solar eclipse. Reading a medicine prescription will never cure the disease until the medicine is taken. Another challenge is managing the addictive nature of instantly gratifying simple pleasures, which can come at the expense of more sustainable and meaningful happiness. Other times we are misled by the hope that happiness will come naturally, after an investment of personal sacrifice in order to obtain the next level of power, money or security. These indirect routes can inadvertently become so circuitous, that we can find ourselves travelling further away from the original objective of happiness. There are, of course, those other times where we manage to stay true to ourselves and feel happy and content with our lives.

This collection of happiness-growing exercises is for all of these scenarios; to guide us down the most direct path of greatest happiness, and to make it enjoyable to dance down too!

Thanks to a natural trait of our brains called neuroplasticity, we can intentionally redirect synapses within the brain to densify those neural pathways which give more desired thought patterns, such as becoming naturally more present, more optimistic, more grateful, and generally happier. This also reduces the influence of undesired thought patterns, meaning we can learn to free ourselves of negativity, regain control over our thoughts and feelings, and chose to live an *even happier* life.

Over countless generations of evolution: from cavemen to modern day, the human mind has been naturally encouraged to react more intensely to negative stimuli. For example, we detect sweet tastes at 1 part per 200, yet can detect bitter at 1 per 2 million, people hate to lose more than they love to win, and we require on average five positive comments to counter one negative comment. These natural reactions have ingrained a deep-rooted "negativity bias" into the emotional and cognitive reactivity of our minds, which is predominantly governed by the part of the brain called the amygdala.

For this reason, powerful doses of the "fight, flight or freeze" hormones like adrenalin and cortisol are released when we encounter a threat, to help us survive in life or death situations. Unfortunately, if these hormones are present for extended periods of time, they can accelerate the ageing process and contribute to many known diseases from heart disease to memory impairment.

So where's the good news? Well, we have already been living with this inherited negativity bias all of our lives, and in the grand scheme of life things aren't usually so bad, right? We can therefore take this starting point and, just like training a muscle to increase specific characteristics of strength, endurance or flexibility, we can train our minds to adopt new thought habit patterns, that enable us to feel *even happier*. We can learn new ways to process everyday thoughts and feelings and increase our capacity for happiness.

This neuroplasticity is often described as "Neural Darwinism", which is a naturally-occurring process within our brains where the brain selectively "prunes" specific synapses, like a gardener prunes a rose bush, and recycles cells and connections in the neural pathways that are less regularly used. It then redirects blood supply, and enhances the density of the synapses in the more active areas of the mind. Hence we can learn to overcome this inherited negativity bias and teach ourselves to feel happier and happier!

Some of the ideas in this book may resonate with you more than others, so however they initially feel to you, take a moment to digest each one. Like planting a seed, let it settle for a while in the garden of your open mind. We never know what may sprout into a fruitful harvest after the nourishing sunlight and rains of life have passed.

When we train a muscle, it gets stronger, when we stretch we become more flexible, and when we exercise and habituate the thought patterns that encourage happiness, we become better at that too. There may be exercises that certain people are not entirely prepared for yet, so like lifting an inappropriately heavy weight at the gym, if something feels it is doing more harm than good, it is absolutely necessary to leave those exercises for when you are better prepared to tackle them.

There may be challenging times through the adventures of our lives, when "choosing" to feel happy seems to be impossibly difficult. If we become transfixed on the ultimate objective, always looking at the distance still to cover, we may become demotivated and risk giving up on the objective believing it is impossibly far away to ever achieve.

So instead of overly focusing on the final objective, if we focus our thoughts, time and efforts on the process, understanding the influencers of happiness and taking action on the small steps we can take, we naturally start progressing toward an *even happier* state of being.

The following pages are filled with actionable steps to guide you towards ever-growing happiness. As we take these steps, we will be gaining a new view of what happiness truly means, and like all good explorers, we'll be creating a map of our journey as we go. With each step, we will better understand the path toward even more happiness, learning how all the pieces of our lives piece together, and how different elements of our mindset and our lifestyle choices can impact our happiness. Imagine, every wonderful element of your life today, getting *even happier*!

Let's begin!

The First Step

Happiness can be thought of as a combined experience of moment to moment joy, contentment, or positive well-being, with a longer term sense that one's life is good, meaningful, and worthwhile.

The moment to moment aspects are processed mostly in the right half of the brain, the "Right Here, Right Now, Right Hemisphere". It is usually relatively easy to identify when we feel joy, gratitude, contentment, pleasure, and identify which stimuli typically make us feel these emotions.

The other component, the greater sense of meaning within a life aligned with one's values, is more subjective and depends more on our individual values. This is often associated with the left hemisphere of the brain, including relationships and memories.

The journey of ever-increasing happiness involves learning to enjoy the moment to moment joyful emotions, while living a lifestyle that provides a sense of meaning behind that enjoyment. Increasing happiness can therefore be influenced by our thought habits, and the actions we take, our lifestyle choices.

So there are really only two types of step we can take, like a left footstep and a right footstep, we either take a step towards a happier mindset, or a step towards a happier lifestyle. We are either learning to experience joy, contentment, and positive well-being, or we are building a lifestyle that is healthy, meaningful, and worthwhile.

Each affects the other, and since thoughts occur before our actions, the mindset is the foundation upon which all happiness is grown. The actions we take, build upon these thoughts. This is the basic environment for happiness.

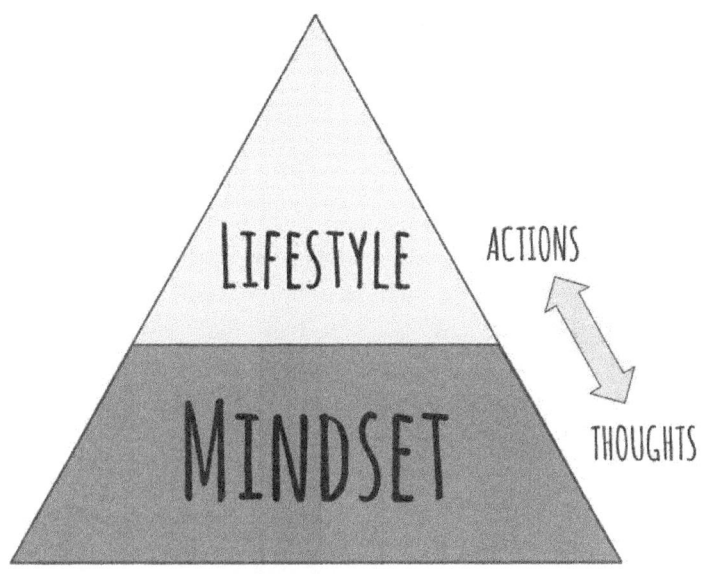

Our thoughts are the basis for all actions, which themselves produce a meaningful life for which we can nurture grateful thoughts and enjoy a meaningful happiness.

As we progress through the steps of this guidebook, we will be gaining an ever clearer view of this pyramid environment. There is no single destination of happiness, it is not something we blindly hope to someday arrive at. Instead, we are learning to develop our understanding of the influencing elements of happiness, the physiology of how happier thoughts and feelings affect our bodies, and how we can develop the skills to make happier thoughts a more regular naturally occurring habit.

Hi there! You'll see this book is split into two halves just like the last diagram. It first dissects the elements of our mindset that influence our happiness, the latter exploring the elements of our lifestyles that influence our happiness. Each chapter introduces a new element of the happiness environment, and each step builds valuable skills within that element. This will all come together by page 107, so let's get going!

Part One:

The Mindset Steps

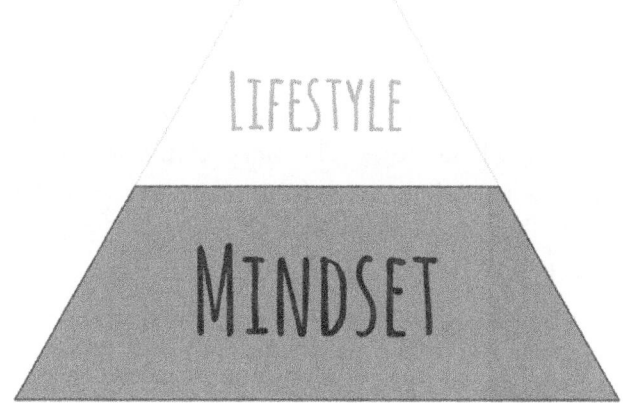

Perspective

2. Things in life either happen **to** us or they happen **for** us. Perspective really does change everything. That doesn't mean that it's always easy to find everything great and wonderful all the time, but it does mean that everything can be accepted, dealt with, overcome, and progressed from.

     Ken Keyes Jr eloquently puts this sentiment in terms of gifts. "*Everything is a gift of the universe — even joy, anger, jealously, frustration, or separateness. Everything is perfect either for our growth or our enjoyment.*"

     Our brains are subjected to constant feeds of sensations, from sights, sounds, and physical sensations from our bodies external environments to thoughts and feelings arising from our internal mental environment. It is how we choose to interpret these sensations that makes all the difference.

     If we are only aware of the most prominent sensations such as very pleasant or very unpleasant feelings, we become oblivious to the less obvious subtleties of our lives and risk being misled into developing an incomplete view of what it means to be conscious. Perceiving also the more subtle sensations, is necessary to develop a truer, more complete understanding of our lives. The story of the four blind men who each believe the part of the elephant that they are touching is the true definition of an elephant, demonstrates how important a complete perspective of the true situation is.

     We can better understand the reality of consciousness and our capacity for happiness through observational meditation practices such as mindfulness, and in the following chapters of this book, we will learn how to develop optimism based on the true reality, not imaginary circumstance.

Our perspective of the world around us and within us, is the fundamental basis for building happiness, as it influences our thoughts and actions. Understanding a healthy perspective, conducive to genuine happiness, is the first region of the happiness map we are chartering, and lies at the base of the pyramid below:

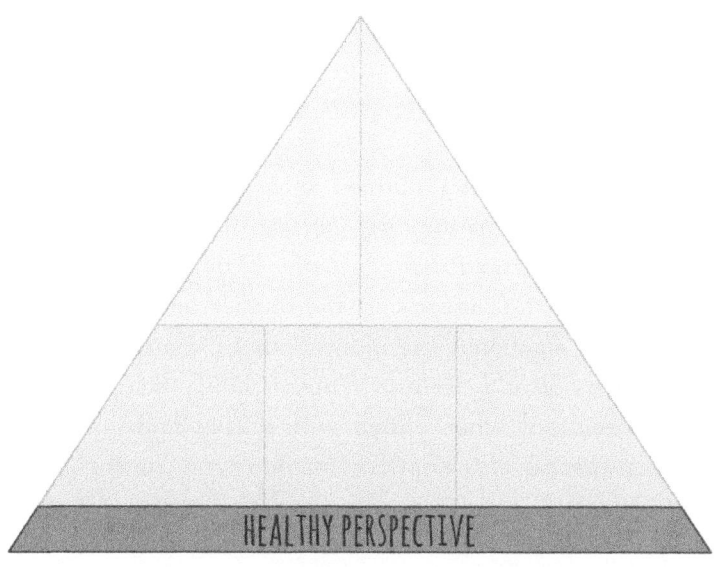

Perspective – The way in which we interpret the events and sensations coming into our minds can change everything.

Hi again! There are a few more steps in the Perspective region of the happiness map before we step into the next area, so let's make sure we build upon a strong and sustainable foundation.

3. "I should do this" or "I should do that". How often have "Should" thoughts got you feeling guilty and stressed about something? These kinds of thoughts don't help us progress toward greater happiness. Feelings of "Should" are inherently de-energising and are negatively framed, automatically triggering an equal and opposite emotional resistance to the thought/task.

It feels like being nagged into action, which no-one responds well to. Instead, we can reframe them as "Could" thoughts. The connotations of "Could" highlights our choice in the matter. "Could", empowers the thinker and removes that paralysing emotional resistance that comes with the guilt-ridden "Should" feelings. These "Could" thoughts can be further beneficial when paired with a brief contemplation of the consequences of the options, meaning we can consider the repercussions of any action or inaction without our judgement being as clouded by our emotional position.

When we practise catching any thoughts involving the sensation of "Should", we can choose to redirect the mind to understand it is merely a choice of options. There's no guilt attached, there's no emotional confusion, it is just a situation with a few probable consequences. We become empowered to make positive, objective decisions to live how we chose to live.

4. Falling into a "The grass is always greener on the other side" mindset can be a dangerous negativity trap! To get out, practise noticing those jealously comparative thoughts, observe their origins and calmly use each thought to motivate an action to water the grass on YOUR side of the fence.

There are of course rare certain situations when we need to take significant action to escape a wholly negative environment. Like taking action to avoid an abusive relationship, end workplace bullying, or leave any other universally detrimental scenarios where the grass really might be greener somewhere else. However, our first objective is always better to have an internal focus. To look at improving our world, not comparing with others, quitting and hoping for the best.

The imagined alternative situations on the other side of the fence will harbour unknown challenges of their own, only knowable when we experience them directly. We can never know if another outcome could be better or worse than our present situation, we can only learn to enjoy the grass we have grown. The story of the Chinese Farmer demonstrates that we can never know the repercussions of any event. It goes like this:

Once there was a Chinese farmer who worked
his poor farm with his son and their horse.
One day, the horse ran off, and neighbours came
and said "How unfortunate for you!".
The farmer was grateful for their concern, but
only replied, "Maybe."

The horse returned the next day, followed by
seven wild horses, the neighbours gathered
again and exclaimed, "What good luck for you!"
The farmer stayed calm and replied: "Maybe".
The next day, while trying to tame one of the
horses, the farmer's son fell off and broke his leg.
"Oh how sad for you!" the neighbours cried.
"Maybe" repeated the farmer.
Shortly thereafter, the local Army conscription
officers came knocking to recruit soldiers to be
sent to battle. Many young men were being
killed, but the farmer's son had a broken leg and
was left at home to recover.
When the people said to the farmer, "What a
good thing your son couldn't fight!"
"Maybe" was all the farmer said.

5. Make your *What if*s, **What is**.

All the "What if" scenarios in our heads — "*What will happen if* this happens in the future?", or "*What if* I had done that thing differently in the past?" — only cloud our proper judgement and can make it far more difficult to obtain sustainable happiness.

If you notice any of these "catastrophizing" thoughts or worries, see what happens if you try to consciously swap every "*What if*" thought with a "**What is**" thought.

Acknowledge the original ruminating thought and question its validity. Ask yourself **What is** the reality of this situation? **What is** known right now? **What is** an option for me at the moment?

In theory, it is a simple mindfulness technique, in practice, it can have a profound positive impact on reducing stress and increasing our control over our emotional well-being. The more we practise anything, the better we become at it, so start with a one-day trial, making a conscious determination to transform all of your *What if*'s, into **What is**. You may find yourself another step or two happier.

6. What is your story? What story do the life-narrating thoughts in your head tell?

Our unassuming little super-brains behind our eyes quietly absorb the seemingly random, seemingly unrelated events of our everyday lives and catalyse it all into a powerful and influential story that dictates our mood, feelings, and beliefs.

Some people's minds create a dramatic story, other people tell themselves their story is one of self-actualisation, growth and love. And sometimes our minds might want to tell us a catastrophic tragedy, that every event of the day was somehow orchestrated to make our lives difficult. A story of struggle and failure. Intentional disruption. Whatever the story is that you tell about yourself, and however far along the story you are, don't make the mistake of thinking you're passive in it.

Our lives don't need to be passively listening to the audiobook of our mind's analyses. We're not the obediently directed characters of a written script, you are writing your story with every conscious moment of your life, and it is your mind that spins the tale.

It might require some practice and positivity training (like we do at A Good Way To Think), to turn the mind into a positivity machine; the first step is remembering that the pen is already in your hand. It's your perspective that changes the world, why not write yourself a great day!

7. Seeing is not always required for believing. When we set out on almost any journey, the journey to work or even to get something from the fridge, we believe we will get there before we see the final destination. As long as we keep on taking actions that progress us in the right direction, if we believe we will get there, we will.

Similarly, do we really need to see the silver lining to every cloud if we truly believe it is there in the first place? How would we feel if we truly believed everything would work out for the best in the end? Perhaps if it hasn't worked out for the best yet, it's not the end yet?

Believe you are pessimistic, and you will become so, believe you are optimistic, and you will become so.

Since all things are impermanent, perhaps so too is our ignorance of how to be even happier. Try to nurture a process-oriented focus, understanding the power of "yet". A goal is never failed, it just hasn't been achieved **yet**.

Think about one meaningful thing that you'd like to achieve but you've just not had the time, the opportunity, the drive, (the limiting belief) to achieve it. Now remind yourself of this goal or hope, and be clear that it hasn't been achieved YET. Just, not yet...

Focus on the process, not the result. Praise the process, praise the efforts and the learning developments, and remove the onus from the "right or wrong" answer. Whatever your hope or dream is; working patiently and diligently, taking action to follow an effective process, you are bound to be successful. The "yet" perspective offers the opportunity to observe one's own improvement without fear of failure as there is no failure with a "yet" attitude. Only success.

I love the power of "yet"! It is one of the most powerful tools in the motivation toolbox. By looking at progress towards our objectives or resolutions in terms of those things we've already achieved and the things that just haven't been achieved yet, success towards anything becomes inevitable! Nothing is a failure, it just might not be a success yet. There is plenty more to explore in this province of Perspective, but for now, let's move into the next part of the map — it's an important one!

Grateful Mindset

8. It turns out it is not happiness that makes us thankful, but thankfulness that makes us happy. Grateful thoughts generate happy feelings. They are the seeds from which all our happiness grows.

Grateful thought patterns activate the brainstem region that produces dopamine, and gratitude, especially with a sense of meaningfulness such as with compassionate love for others, increases brain activity in social dopamine circuits, which makes social interactions noticeably more enjoyable. Gratitude also increases serotonin production in the anterior cingulate cortex, the most influential neurotransmitter involved in our feelings of happiness.

We cannot always dictate our emotional well-being and choose to be happy, the reality of life is often too volatile for such an easy solution. Instead, through their inseparable cause and effect relationship, we can learn to increase our faculty for gratitude, planting seeds of grateful thoughts throughout the mind, such that they naturally grow into meaningful and rewarding fields of genuine happiness.

Since gratitude is the precursor of happiness, it is the central foundation of the happiness landscape and is directly connected to every other happiness-related element. In many ways, the other components we will later cover, only positively influence our happiness when combined with gratitude.

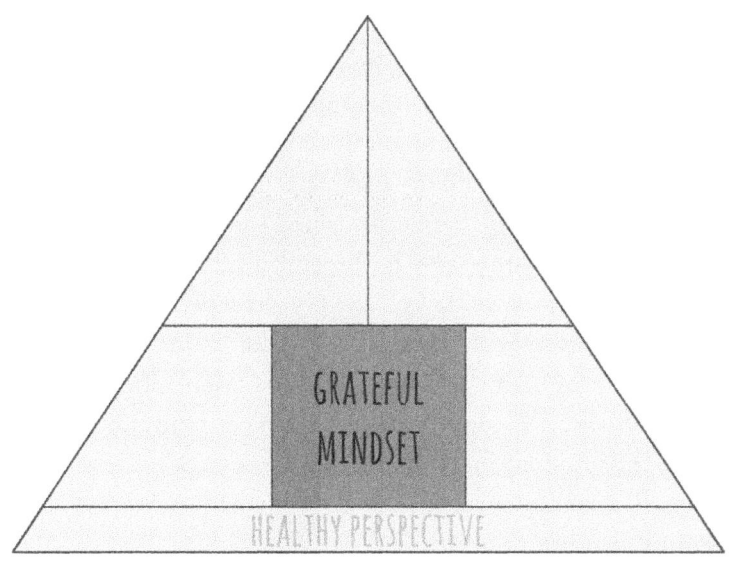

Developing a Grateful Mindset – Directly connected to everything that positively influences happiness, gratitude is the central foundation lasting happiness.

9. Many people maintain a journal in which they write down the things for which they are grateful. It can be a really simple exercise, like identifying three good things that are in your life today, or listing five things you are grateful happened today, and has been shown to provide both an immediate and lasting effect on happiness.

In a 2012 study[1] from Reed College and the University of California, leading positive psychologists tested this strategy in an online setting and found that the benefits lasted as long as six months. A small uptick for six months in return for just five minutes of writing is a pretty good deal!

If you've not tried a gratitude journal before, try it out today! If you don't have a notebook or a phone to record them physically, then just mentally create a short list of at least five things you are grateful for, and be specific! You could do this before falling asleep each day or before getting up in the morning, while brushing your teeth or while resting in the sanctity of a bathroom! It has been found to be even more effective to physically record these personal sources of happiness somewhere. The main objective is training the mind to practise gratitude more often, and the records will also become a mini happiness fountain that you can return to in tougher times in future.

These sentences could be a great framework for a gratitude journal of your own:

Right now, I'm feeling _____.

I'm really glad I can _____.

I'm lucky I have _____ and _____ and _____.

A mini-miracle I saw recently was _____.

With freedom to think my own thoughts and make my own decisions, I can _____ and _____ and _____ and _____! How incredibly lucky!

Right now, I am right here, and I feel _____

10. A great way to increase our capacity and regularity of feeling happy and grateful is by practising verbalising your gratitude every day. Make a pledge to yourself now that whenever you feel grateful for something or someone, you will tell someone! You could tell anyone, the important thing is to put that feeling into words and share the grateful sentiment.

"Gratitude unlocks the fullness of life. It turns what we have into enough, and more. It turns denial into acceptance, chaos to order, confusion to clarity. It can turn a meal into a feast, a house into a home, a stranger into a friend. Gratitude makes sense of our past, brings peace for today, and creates a vision for tomorrow."

—Melody Beattie

11. Periods of "deprivation" are recommended by almost all happiness experts to heighten and deepen the sensations of appreciation and gratitude upon return of the deprived thing. All major religions recognise the benefits of temporary deprivation and annually encourage their community

members to follow a period of temporary deprivation, such as Lent (Christianity), Ramadan (Islam), Yom Kippur (Judaism), and Maha Shivaratri (Hinduism), among others.

These practices have been shown to give lasting boosts in happiness, attributed to the increased gratitude we feel for things once they are back.

12. Another great exercise to increase our capacity for gratitude (and hence our capacity for happiness), is to challenge yourself to start at least 10 sentences each day with "Thank you for …". You could set a reminder on your phone 10 times per day, or keep scores with friends or colleagues.

People who say thank you more are generally happier people. So are those who frequently discuss and write about what they're thankful for, so why not see if you can hit 10 Thank You's today, and see if this increased awareness of gratitude brings you some happiness too!

13. When you next notice a positive thought or a moment of joy, or gratitude, or happiness, just see what happens when you follow this two step "**Explore and Communicate**" exercise:

Step 1: **Explore** – After noticing you are experiencing a pleasant moment, a joyful feeling or a happy thought, bring all your attention to the boundless positive aspects of it, take a step back to marvel and admire how wonderful the moment is to even exist. What miraculous sequence of good fortune was necessary to create that moment, that feeling, that thought? Delve into it with the curiosity of a child seeing her first rainbow.

Step 2: **Communicate** – Now we're appreciating something beautiful, double the enjoyment by sharing it with someone else! If you've enjoyed feeling exceptionally "upbeat" for some reason, tell someone! If a good deed was done to you, and you've filled yourself with gratitude, let the happiness continue to multiply by sharing your feelings with at least one other person. Whatever happiness you have just explored, multiply the positive impact by communicating it to someone else.

Not only is it great practice identifying moments of positive thoughts, revisiting the positive moment doubles its impact by doubling the neural activity through the grateful synapses of the brain as we relive the enjoyable moment in our mind. The communication phase may even highlight more reasons to feel grateful for the happy moment. Reflecting on happier moment also increases the quality of retention of the memories, and will also positively influence the relationship with the person you communicated with. This is thanks to the "Spontaneous trait transference" effect, which we'll get to on step 85.

Mental strength requires **Power** to resist negativity, Flexibility to view positivity in all situations, and Endurance to persevere through challenges. A cleaner mind also allows for both more regular, and deeper sensations of happiness.

Positive Thoughts

We mentioned our inherited negativity bias at the start of the book, and that there are exercises we can do to train the mind balance itself with a more positive nature. As we deepen our understanding of gratitude (and subsequent happiness), we can increase the opportunities for gratitude by nurturing more positive thoughts.

These steps are about increasing the quantity of uplifting and emotionally rewarding thoughts, as well as the depth and intensity of their positivity. Nurturing more positive thoughts also involves allowing the negative thoughts to loosen their grip on us by learning how to cope with the negative thinking habits we may have inherited or developed through life so far.

This is the third region of the happiness map, and the steps we take here are pivotal in feeding the grateful mindset element with reasons to cultivate gratitude, and opportunities to feel *even happier!*

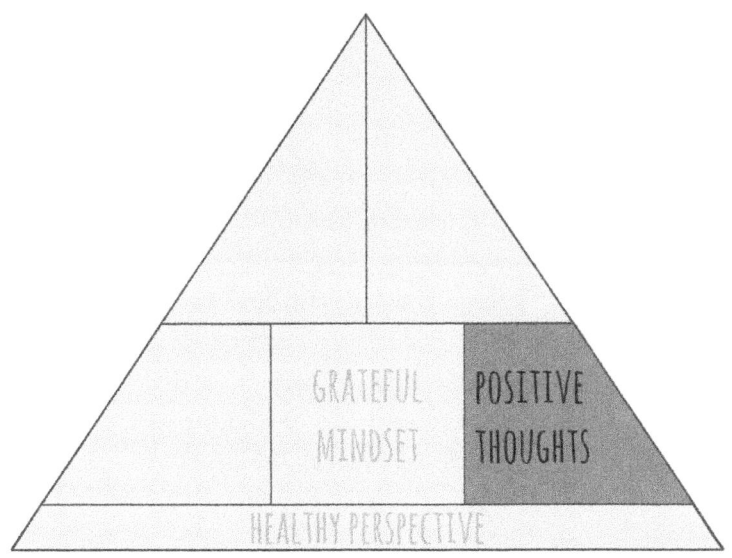

Positive Thoughts – the area of happiness including managing negative thinking patterns, and increasing the frequency and intensity of positive thoughts like joy and contentment.

14. Some people's thoughts tend to be more negative than positive, and for other people, the opposite is true. So how can we ensure we get to and stay in the second group of mostly positive thinkers? Our thoughts typically spawn from subconscious questions, for example, a negatively biased mind might initiate thoughts with questions like:

What will I do if this or that unwanted thing happens?
Why does this always happen to me?
Why can't I do this?

The conscious mind will then be neutral in answering our questions as this becomes conscious thought. It looks at all the evidence in our experience banks and creates the subsequent thought. Negatively oriented questions mean negative oriented thoughts. So the key is to train the mind to ask better questions... Questions like:

What's great about this?
Why is this exactly what I need?
What will I be able to learn from this?
What am I most proud of about my
[business, family, week, hobby]?

When we catch a negative thought, especially a negatively posed question, try to reframe the underlying question into a more positive orientation and ask it again. Positive questions lead to uplifting, motivating answers, and hence happier thoughts, feelings, actions, and everything else that follows! Try to keep catching the negative thoughts, reconsider the question and allow the possibility of something positive. You can also intentionally ask yourself positively framed questions throughout the day, to encourage those questions to arise more regularly naturally.

We can learn to be more optimistic, and can learn to be even happier. It all starts with the right questions.

15. One popular and effective exercise developed by *A Good Way To Think* is called the **"Reinterpretation of Past Events"** exercise.

We start this exercise by considering an event from the past, perhaps something without too much emotional attachment at first, and in a calm place, free from interruption and distraction, we spend just a couple of minutes mentally exploring some of the potentially positive outcomes from that event. We can reflect on the new information we obtained through the experience, the lessons learned that could help us in the future if a similar situation were to occur. We can consider whether the event created an opportunity for fresh new beginnings, did it open unexpected pathways? Did it motivate some progressive or remedial action, or spark a more enjoyable event thereafter?

Take a few minutes to think about the event and answer positively oriented questions like those in the previous step:

"What was great about this?
Why was that exactly what I needed?
What else did I learn from this?"

With time and practice we can increase our aptitude for reconsidering the past, and over time, as we rewire the synapses, one neuron at a time, we learn how to revisit increasingly recent and increasingly emotionally challenging events, and learn to find good in them too. The more we practise tuning the mind to focus on positive outcomes, the more positive outcomes we find.

We incrementally become ever-more capable of processing emotionally difficult situations in real-time, as they are happening. It is very important to accept that being human and being happy includes accepting the full spectrum of human emotions, without becoming overpowered by any one of them, including negativity. It may exist, and we can accept its existence to regain power over it. Negative feelings may exist, but so also can so many positive ones. We can practise training the mind to increase control of the thoughts, allowing for an even happier and more positive life.

This learned optimism is pursuant to the modern scientific research of positive psychology, which demonstrates that the majority of our capacity for happiness and "positive affect" comes from learnable skills.

16. We can take this positive shifting to the next level whenever something "bad" seems to have happened to us. We can first take a moment to acknowledge which thought reactions and feelings are generated by the initial situation, and just observe what internal reaction this creates. Instead of trying to change or suppress any strong feelings about it, acknowledge the thoughts that exist, and then like putting a naughty child in a "time-out zone", don't feed the thought with further attention.

How can we do this? Firstly by noticing if we are starting to feed it. We can feed the negativity if we start thinking about how we should have acted differently, or when we repeat the story to others, telling them what annoyance we encountered today at work, or sharing an aggravating anecdote.

Secondly, if you notice you are starting to feed the negativity, instead of trying to stop the thought from existing, we can interrupt that thought and redirect it towards something more positive. This could take the form of appreciating of some other element of today that was pleasant or enjoyable. The negative thought will be starved of attention and reduces in influence significantly. Whenever it may arise again, replace the negative feelings again. The last time you laughed, an achievement you're proud of, a relationship you cherish. By starving the negativity of fuel it will soon fade out completely.

This incrementally helps rewire the inherited negatively-biased synapses, facilitating greater capacity for self-cultivated "neutral" or "positive-biased" thought patterns, through the wonderful neuroplastic powers of the brain. These happier thoughts are also linked with positive hormone and endorphin releases. This is a great exercise, just remember that awareness and acceptance of thoughts does not mean suppressing them and ignoring them; some causes of negative thoughts may be helpful indicators of opportunities for improvement, highlighting the need to make a change. Accepting these thoughts includes accepting the responsibility to take action.

So through all those interruptions of life, complications to your peacefulness, undesirable events and inconvenient changes to your ideal day – things just happen, remember they either happen **to** you or they happen **for** you.

Which fire will you feed?

17. Another simple mindset shift can come from changing the low energy "**Have To**" thoughts into higher energy "**Get To**" thoughts. Try to first notice any situations where you may feel forced into a situation, with little control or choice. Maybe you're swept into the autopilot routine and the thought arises, "I have to pick up the kids!". Reframing this

into a grateful and positive "I get to pick up the kids" might just take things a small step in the happier direction.

18. Challenge yourself to "Communicate the Positives" for a day. The rules are simple:
    1. If you experience a positive emotion such as enthusiasm or joy; or a loving thought such as gratitude, you must tell someone about it!
    2. If you have a nice conversation or delightful encounter with someone, tell someone else about it!
    3. If you notice a conversation has led to a negative place, be the person to redirect it towards a positive, uplifting topic — how about telling them something from rule 1 or 2?

    Try this exercise for a day and be aware of how it makes you feel. Is it exhausting or energising, embarrassing or empowering, isolating or connecting?

19. Celebrate small wins by using physical gestures and reactions to maximise the effect of uplifting feelings. Whether it's fist pumping the air, smiling gleefully with eyebrows and all, or jumping up and down like you've won the lottery, physical celebrations release powerful joyous hormones that do us a world of good. They accentuate the good feelings by increasing the intensity of happy hormones in the blood, which also accelerates the habit forming processes that tune our minds into the other celebratory moments throughout the adventures of life.

Small wins can be anything potentially progressive towards something meaningful, from receiving an act of kindness to noticing a blessing. There are countless moments of small progression each day that we can learn to enjoy when we become more aware of them. Sequences of small wins can punctuate the day with moments of happiness, and celebrating them with physical actions makes them ever more prominent and memorable. This practice also encourages the mind to become more aware of positive and enjoyable circumstances in the future. What a win!

20. Life can sometimes be an unpredictable adventure of emotional turmoil. When things seem to be going wrong and you are facing personal failure, remember these three questions to ask yourself. They remind us of the progressive nature of failure, and how to enjoy fun of failure when something inevitably doesn't go how we had hoped it would:

1. What is my goal?
2. If I honestly accept I may fail, why should I carry on?
3. What is the alternative?

Just remember: if something is truly worth doing, it is still worth doing badly. We can fail at the things we don't like, or we can fail at the things we do... but one of those is not really a failure at all.

21. It is easy to forget, but there is only good in this world; evil does not exist. Every human action is, at its most basic level, motivated by our desire to be liberated from suffering, either in the present moment and/or the future. All of our actions stem from this desire to somehow obtain a lasting sense of peaceful happiness.

There can of course appear to be a lack of good in people, and occasionally sure, people may act from misguided fear and ignorance, not knowing how best to achieve that deepest innate desire to be truly happy, free from all suffering.

Since the only active force that drives us to action originates from a good place, when events appear to be in conflict with our desire for suffering-free happiness, such as a person saying or doing something we find hurtful, we can safeguard our happiness by applying the law of **Acceptance and Nonresistance**. With a nonresistant, accepting approach, we can transform the actions of the "enemy" into opportunities to learn and benefit.

We start by accepting that their actions were based on their thoughts, which were assumed from their experiences, and those experiences will inevitably be very different to our own. At their most fundamental motivating root however, we all share that same objective.

These challenging situations are offering us an opportunity to be more understanding, to practise being more loving in the face of fear, and a chance to learn from the decisions of others. Acceptance includes accepting responsibility to use this opportunity to learn and progress. Accepting that we must take action to maintain our happiness, such as increasing our happiness skills with the other steps within this guidebook. By not resisting supposedly evil actions, the perpetrator is immediately disarmed and serves only to benefit us by offering an opportunity to practise this exercise, to practise patience, and to practise compassion. Just like physical exercises, it's the tougher exercises that give the most results. We can even thank our "evil perpetrators" for offering us the opportunity to develop our happiness skills. This is the sentiment intended by the phrase "Love your enemies" (Luke 6:27 and Matthew 5:44). Who knows, they may even learn from the situation themselves.

So evil doesn't really exist at all, it just can appear that way when we are unaware of how to achieve genuine lasting happiness. If you think about life in that way; that every human action, although sometimes ignorant, is motivated by good, it can certainly feel like a pretty amazing place we get to share for a while.

In 2005, researchers from the universities of California, Missouri and Illinois published a meta-analysis² of 225 academic studies concluding that "happiness is associated with and precedes numerous successful outcomes, as well as behaviors paralleling success." Happier employees were on average 31% more productive, recorded 37% higher sales, and were three times more creative! These profound results are partnered with reduced stress, which improves our problem-solving abilities and allows for better rational decision making!

22. Getting enough sleep can be a big happiness booster in the short, medium and long term. Almost all adults need at least seven hours each night, often significantly more, to cognitively function effectively, so try not to kid yourself about how much sleep you need! Adequate sleep helps us to form memories and reduce stress hormones, which are notoriously combative against happiness. In one study[3] at UC Berkeley, when viewing a range of images described as neutral to disturbing, sleep deprived subjects in the trial became 60% more reactive to negative pictures compared to subjects who were well rested.

Sleep allows us retain control of the thoughts, so instead of our minds having a mind of their own, we can allow ourselves to regain control and to choose happiness, to thrive, physiologically and neurologically.

23. Consumer advertising is designed to encourage us to compare ourselves with others and tries to make us feel dissatisfied with what we have. Comparisons like this can really hinder happiness!

We can stop these happiness leeches in their tracks by actively reducing our exposure to advertising – muting the TV when ads come on, installing ad blockers to internet browsers, and choosing to replace the times we look at billboards, tabloids, games and magazines with books, hobbies, friends' faces and nature. We can even redirect conversations that drift into the toxic realms of comparisons towards lighter subjects. If someone wants to talk enviously of what someone else has, redirect the conversation towards something you do have.

If comparisons become absolutely unavoidable, try instead to develop a "**Selective Social Comparison**". That means instead of comparing yourself with more financially wealthy, "beautiful" or famous people, select the opposite 1% of society, the oppressed, trapped, fearful, uneducated souls of humanity, and balance the comparisons. It is certainly best to avoid all comparisons entirely, but *selective social comparisons* can be a stepping stone in the right direction.

Ultimately we can try to turn comparisons into opportunities for gratitude, choosing not to focus on what is missing from our lives but being grateful for the abundance that is present.

24. The most effective way to increase our happiness is to focus on wellness, not illness, to nurture positive thoughts and habits instead of trying to remove negative ones. This positive orientation is an effective method for many self-improvement goals from stopping smoking to losing weight, and is extremely effective for increasing happiness!

So instead of focusing on reducing something undesired by trying not to think the undesired thoughts or perform the undesired habit, try a positively oriented approach. Knowing that there are only 24 hours in a day, if we can try to squeeze in additional activities that are desired, which encourage positive thoughts and sensations, the other unwanted thoughts and moments will have no opportunity to arise and have to make way for the higher priority thoughts. Slowly, the re-prioritised activities and corresponding better thoughts become natural lifestyle choices and hard-wired thinking habits, resulting in an incrementally happier life.

This is the same theory as white water rafters use to follow the safest parts of the river – they don't stare at all the dangerous rocks, they use the flow of the river to find a safe passage. The same is true for mountain bikers following a narrow, rocky trail, even if cliffs drop away from either side, the rider doesn't feed the fear by paying attention to the precipice, she focuses on doing everything she can to follow the safe trail, paying so much attention to the rideable part of the mountain that nothing else seems to exist. There is only the bike and the trail. No cliffs, no fear, just finding every inch of happiness, among a terrain of unhelpful distractions.

25. One great little happiness booster is to practise **Celebrating Progress**, regardless of however small the progress seems to be! This is like celebrating small wins, but can still be done if nothing is completed or resolved. If you see something in your life develop in a productive or meaningful way, even if it is microscopic progress, then acknowledge the progress, be grateful for it and celebrate it! Congratulations, you're already a quarter of the way through this book, you know more now than you did yesterday!

By habituating these moments of joy, the increased levels of serotonin and dopamine accelerate the speed at which neural connections are made and pruned (Neural Darwinism), which in turn accelerates the neuroplastic effect of getting better at the task (spotting and celebrating positive progression) in the future. It also exercises the reward systems, motivating us for further progress and increasing our capacity to feel accomplished.

26. Being micro-ambitious can boost your happiness and productivity! Micro-ambition is a momentum building mindset where we dedicate all efforts on the microscopic goal of achieving something right in front of us, right in the very moment, and celebrating its completion. Then we take the next micro-goal and hit it with all our focus. Remember to celebrate when it is done too! Your first micro-goal could be to finish reading this sentence, the next could be to smile!

27. Here's a super quick, and super awesome little step. Take the next 20 seconds to imagine the best possible outcome for today. Imagine it going awesomely! Try to focus less on specific tasks or events happening that may be beyond your control and more on the things within your control, like your mindset, your enthusiasm, your compassion and your patience. You could imagine being super productive, as patient as a saint, or use the 20 seconds to project your mind to your future self this evening, where you might see yourself feeling accomplished and grateful that you had remembered to be humble and positive all day!

Imagine, and truly visualise today going brilliantly. Being the person you are proud to be, acting how you would like to act, and see what happens.

28. Try to encourage **Positively Framed Communication.** Instead of responding to a favour request with a negatively framed answer, such as: "No, not until after lunch", we can reframe it more positively into something like "Yes, we can do that straight after lunch".

It is a simple trick that works astonishingly well for the progression of the conversation by maintaining a positive atmosphere between the conversation participants, and keeps your mind positive with feelings of 'Yes', instead of distracted by the energy-sapping connotations of repeating 'No'. Children also respond significantly better to positively framed responses.

29. Speaking of the power of positively oriented words, let's see what happen trying out this simple, joyful mantra. Take your time and don't worry about how silly you think you look or sound, just repeat the words below, slowly, and **with intent**, either out loud or if you'd rather, just listen to each word via the reading voice in your head. With no thoughts of expectation or anticipation, focus only on the words and their meaning. You can repeat the general mantra for as long as you like:

YES. YES, YES, YES, YES, YES. YES. YES, YES, YES, YESS!

Then have some fun with it, try words that have happy emotional connotations, like SMILE, HAPPY, I CAN, or LOVE. Try to connect with the words, and engage their emotive connotations of positive affirmation. More energy invested will lead to more energy flowing out.

30. Optimism has been linked to a multitude of positive emotional responses in the body, which in turn increase both our capacity for optimistic thought as well as the chances of more favourable outcomes in the first place. This is due to optimistic emotional responses leading to things like lowering stress hormones, which enables better decision making, improved focus and increased motivation, so we can proactively make a more favourable future for ourselves.

Essentially, if we *pretend* to be optimistic, we *become* more optimistic, and inevitable prove our optimism right! To help habituate a more positive mindset, every time you notice a comment leaving your lips that is based on fear and anger, instead of love and understanding, try to follow it immediately with a more loving "positive" comment. If you can notice how they both made you feel this will further accelerate to habit forming process.

This process of turning accidental negatives into intentional positives leaves the more positive thought at the forefront of your conscious mind, influencing future memories of the situation, improving hormone regulation at that moment, and helping to change the natural thought habits of the mind to rebalance the negativity bias to a healthier equilibrium. Whatever you say on any given day, you'll end up feeling great about it!

In the next region of this happiness increasing journey we will be stepping up our faculty of awareness, which when combined with encouraging positive thoughts from this chapter, will unlock innumerable additional mood boosts that can empower us to feel *EVEN HAPPIER* than before!

Live Now, Mindfully

It is only the present moment that exists and the present moment that we can experience, feel positive in, feel grateful in, and feel happy in. The past and future exist only as mental fabrications, as memories and dreams. The laws of nature stop us from physically accessing any previous or future time – they exist only as thoughts accessed from the current now, so a healthy mental time perspective is, therefore, a critical element of the journey to increasing happiness.

Understanding the past and future don't exist, can help liberate us from the influences of regret, guilt, worry or fear, and helps us to return to the contents of this current moment, where we can take the necessary actions to feel *even happier*.

Mindful awareness of the present moment is more than just accepting our present emotions nonjudgmentally. It also involves developing an acute awareness of the sensations of the body, including all the natural the thoughts and feelings.

It is our awareness of the now that provides the opportunity for all gratefully happy thoughts to exists. It is only through increasing our mindfulness of this moment that we can realise both **why** to feel happier, and **how** to feel happier. Positive, mindful thoughts provide us with reasons to feel gratitude, enabling us to feel happier more regularly and intensely. Each of these mindset elements are dependent on the others to maximise happiness.

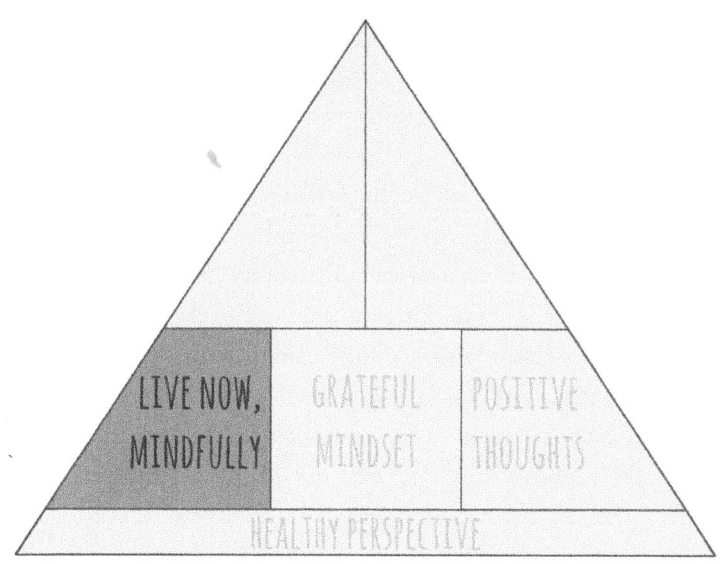

The next element in our Happiness Map is developing awareness of the present moment with equanimity to its true contents. See glossary for more on equanimity.

Accepting the importance of a present mind is a valuable first step in this area, but internalising and indoctrinating this mentality requires a significant investment of time and effort. Like learning any new skill our minds are capable of habituating increasing amounts of present and mindful thoughts. As the mind becomes more aware, it naturally identifies more positive emotions and grateful thoughts, which are what makes us feel happy! This is the fundamental and vital process of creating happiness. We'll see how all the pieces in this pyramid fit together later, let's first learn how to mindfully walk the steps through this present moment!

31. When we feel joyful, we laugh, and when we laugh, we actually start to feel more joyful. This is due to a lifetime of laughter and happy emotions coexisting at the same time. They have become physiologically connected – the mind associates the action with the feeling, and the feeling with the action. This is where advancements in behavioural psychology and neuroscience get really interesting. It has been shown that we can intentionally create these links between behaviour and feeling, and can do far more than Pavlov's famous bell experiment with his salivating dogs.

Through a process now regularly branded as NLP, we can make almost any routine task automatically trigger a specific thought, such as being aware of our thoughts and feelings at this moment, or to feel grateful, happy, positive and so on. NLP stands for Neuro-Linguistic Programming, which is an approach that has revolutionised modern habit oriented mindset-improvements.

We trigger desired thoughts (such as awareness of the present moment) from actions we perform by intentionally linking the action and thought in the same way smiling and joy are connected – repetition.

A great example of this is to attach a "moment of mindfulness" note above the sink where you brush your teeth, on a mirror most regularly gazed in, or at a workplace where a specific action is undertaken. As the action of brushing teeth or looking at oneself in the mirror, or the specific task at work, is undertaken, follow the advice of the note and try to become aware of the sensations of the body and the thoughts in the mind. How do you feel right now?

After much time is invested in this, the mind will begin to automatically associate the action with those thoughts, such that every time you wash your hands, every time the teeth are brushed or the action is taken, the mind becomes present, aware, mindful.

These action-thought connections may require repetition and patience to habituate but can be used to trigger any desired thoughts, such as any of the other 99 steps in this guidebook. When the connection is made, as often as the trigger task is performed, so often you will develop happier thoughts!

32. The *Arrival Fallacy* is the belief that when we arrive at a certain destination, we will be happy, as opposed to focussing on enjoying the progression towards the destination.

The problem with this destination-based approach, is that although we may enjoy the anticipation of future happiness, its arrival rarely makes us as happy as we had expected. By the time we have arrived at the destination, we were already expecting to reach it, so it has already been incorporated into our happiness, reducing much of the surprise. The arrival of the next chapter often then brings additional unanticipated work and responsibility; having a baby, getting a promotion, buying a house etc., is more likely to intensify the mix of emotions already present, than unlock lasting peaceful happiness.

By making sacrifices now in the hope of an uncontrollable future event, we jeopardise both our current and future happiness. Circumstances can change and the future achievement may become insignificant. During the approach of goal attainment, the goal posts often move as we become dedicated to a new, more challenging goal, toward which more short-term sacrifices are made. This arrival fallacy often stems from our desire for more. More recognition, more money, more security, and most importantly, more happiness

But having direction in life and using motivational milestones can help us feel a sense of meaning, or of being part of something bigger than just one lost human soul. The solution therefore, is to take pleasure in the progression towards goal achievement, known as "*Pre-goal-attainment positive affect*". This is finding ways to take pleasure from the atmosphere of growth... To remind ourselves that the journey is more important than the destination... To be aware of the steps we take, the progression, the moment.

The arrival fallacy doesn't mean that pursuing goals isn't a route to happiness, it certainly can help with many elements of happiness, it is just that the goal attainment cannot come with the sacrifice of present moment happiness. If we cannot find happiness in the present moment, nothing we can achieve in the future will bring happiness.

Friedrich Nietzsche words this sentiment as:

"The end of a melody is not its goal; but nonetheless, if the melody had not reached its end it would not have reached its goal either. A parable"

33. In a similar way, a happy life is like a piece of music. The objective of a good piece of music isn't to rush to the end to play the final resolving note, nor is it about speeding through the introduction, or any other part, to get to the chorus or next song as soon as possible.

Likewise, a life can't be fully enjoyed if it is spent rushing through school to get to college; rushing through college to get to university; rushing through that to start a job to earn money to buy a house, a car, holidays and toys; anticipating the glorious next step, the next promotion, the next pay rise, greater recognition, accomplishment, retirement; and then hopefully either the next reincarnation, or reaching heaven.

If music was just about reaching the end, it would be a messy race of lost sounds. But we learn to savour and appreciate as it unfolds, enjoying both the progression and the journey. We already know the basics of how to live to be even happier. Sometimes it is nice to hear a good piece of music to remind us how to do it again.

34. Conscious breathing is the most commonly practised stress reduction technique and has been recognised for thousands of years as an effective way to calm the mind and allow healthier and more uplifting thoughts to arise. In the ancient Pali language, which is used widely within traditional Buddhist texts, this type of meditation is called *Anapanasati* meditation. Anapanasati can be practised by focusing the mind on the sensations created by the breath. It could be as wide a focus as scanning through the body for all movement related to the breath such as the expansion and contraction of the rib cage, the rise and fall of the shoulders, the relaxation of every exhale; or can more targeted, such as focusing intently on the subtle sensations of the breath as it passes through the nostrils and over the moustache area. By focusing on such a small area with more subtle sensations, the mind

becomes sharpened in its awareness of the sensory inputs it is receiving in this present moment.

If a dedicated meditation practice is still too far out of your comfort zone, why not start with this simple conscious breathing exercise and see if it gives your curiosity some confidence:

Try to focus your attention on the sensations generated by the flow of air passing the pathways to reach the lungs, and observe these sensations without the desire to change or modify anything. Simply be aware and observe. After a few breaths, you can return to whatever feels most appropriate to do next.

The increasing oxygen levels in the blood actively reduce the stress hormones cortisol and epinephrine and purge them from our system via the long exhales.

Wherever and whenever the stress hormones need to be put back in their place, practise taking three, long, conscious breaths, and return the clarity and beauty of this present moment. Now is the perfect opportunity to feel happy.

35. Busy modern lives often get us running on a mentally distant, relatively unobservant "autopilot mode". One great way to train ourselves to snap out of this "default mode", is to set a couple of reminders to buzz at various times in the day, with a message to come back from autopilot into the moment, such as:

"Pause a moment",
"Remember you are breathing!",
or
"Stop and smell the roses of life for a moment"

As Ferris Bueller puts it, *"Life moves pretty fast. If you don't stop and look around once in awhile, you could miss it."* If we only get one go at life, it would surely be a shame to miss it, but with a little practice to encourage present thought habits like this, you might start to become more awake to the treasures of life more regularly and see new reasons to be happy more often.

36. Right now, in this beautiful moment, you're going to notice something nice. When you've read this step, put aside the book and take a moment to look around you. Find something beautiful or emotionally valuable to you that is present in your daily life.

    Keep focusing on it until you feel some emotional response to your awareness of this thing. Maybe it has been a while since you last admired it with such intent.

    Keep observing, until a subtle feeling of happiness begins to grow and grow into a thought, emotion or feeling. Continue growing this for a moment longer, becoming aware of the specific thoughts that this thing has inspired in you. How simply noticing it and appreciating it, can make you feel.

    If it will not last forever, remember that it is this impermanent nature that makes the present moment so much more valuable.

37. Clicking big felt tip pen lids... Feeling the sound of the "click" being born, bouncing through the atoms of the air and how it

travels into your ear. The journey across the world the pen has made. Where the oil was extracted, cracked for fuels, processed as plastic, coloured and moulded. Consider the pressure through your thumb. How the muscles tense and the bones absorb the forces. How the sound competes with the rich soundscape around us. The thoughts that arise from the sensory input.

Practising mindfulness may not sound productive in our busy lives, but this type of exercise can increase the efficiency of the functioning brain. By practising mindfulness we can learn to experience the world on a more sensationally rich level, generating countless new opportunities to generate gratitude and happiness. Look small, look large, the cells in the grain of the wood, the life-giving magic of sunlight, does it have texture, rigidity, warmth or conductivity, what other properties? Is it impermanent? Look like a child, non-judgmentally admiring the intricacies of life.

Only you will ever live your life and only you will experience it. It becomes ever more rich and enjoyable through a more aware and appreciative perspective.

I'm a big fan of mindfulness! It is great to practise being mindful both formally through meditation and informally through becoming more aware of our sensory inputs. I wonder, what's the most distant sound you can hear? And where's the tingliest part of your body? Can you taste anything? Can you feel your heart beating? Shut your eyes and see what sensations you uncover.

38. Contrary to popular belief, neither female nor male brains can perform *complex* multitasking. Instead, the brain switches its focus from one activity to another, involving around 0.2 seconds between the activities where it is focusing on neither.

  During this transition phase the brain releases a small hit of dopamine, which is part of the reward system and is often why we find starting new tasks, new projects, and distractions and procrastinations so much more appealing than focusing on a single task to completion.

  Unfortunately, this dopamine hit, whilst mildly pleasurable, can distract from our longer term goals, our ability to focus, and our ability to regulate thoughts healthily. Fortunately for us, there are things we can do to help our minds think more effectively!

  Understanding the nature of the mind is a good start, in this case practising exercises like mindfulness, and more formal meditation practices can increase our ability to focus and execute tasks efficiently, and even increase our productivity and creativity [4, 21].

39. Have you ever made a list of things that you personally find nice? The process of thinking about things that give us some degree of pleasure directly stimulates the brain to synthesise the feelings of interacting with the pleasing thing and activates the brain's pleasure receptors! That means when we imagine enjoying some nice thing (without actually doing anything more than imagining it), our brains synthesise the experience making us feel good! When you've got a nice list together, which may have already made you smile just

coming up with items, you can then try and fill your life with more of the things on your "nice things" list!

Here are a few ideas that might help get you thinking down a nice track:

People watching in the arrivals lounge at airports,
Writing on a banana skin,
The sound of stones bouncing over a frozen lake,
Stretching out as long as you like when yawning,
The heat from a good fire,
Putting on a hot thick jumper when you are cold,
Popping bubble wrap,
Noticing natural beauty,
Treading on crunchy autumn leaves,
Cutting blu-tack with scissors,
Accomplishing something difficult,
Kissing a baby's head,
The cool side of the pillow...

40. The next time you notice a gust in the wind, use the opportunity to practise your mindfulness. Feel the air pass over your skin and let it fill your lungs. Become aware of the sensations of it touching any areas of exposed skin, and the pressure changes upon your clothes. Feel the hairs sway and dance to the natural flow of Earth's energy. Try not to judge and categorise the sensations as enjoyable or good, undesired or bad. They are just sensations that can bring the mind back to the present moment. Training the mind to become aware of the sensations is one of the best ways to return the thoughts to matters of happiness and enjoying the journey.

As we learned in step 34, training the mind to develop awareness of the breath is the most practised technique for increasing one's capacity to appreciate the present moment and dates back many thousands of years. Practising with the more obvious sensations of the wind is a great exercise to start triggering those present moment thoughts and habituate the redistribution of past regrets and future worries back into present moment awareness, gratitude and therefore happiness.

41. Sometimes there is so much going on in our heads that it can make feeling happy seem like we are chasing a Golden Snitch!

How can we possibly get back that clear mind? To be on top of our thoughts and in control of the mind is to get all the view-obscuring clutter out of the way, so we can take a step back to see the bigger picture.

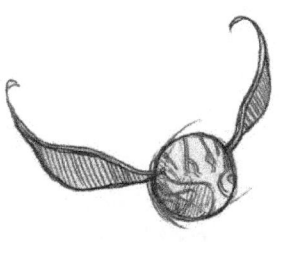

A nice first step to get rid of the distracting thoughts and closer to mental serenity starts by putting pen to paper and writing. No editing, no reviewing it afterwards, you don't even need to write neatly. Just dump it all out. Type your mind into a computer keyboard if it works better for you than a pen and paper. Just allow all the mind clouds to rain through your words and leave behind only a bright and clear mind.

Then, since things rarely go as well in reality as in the theory, breathe three slow conscious breaths, focusing intently on the sensations of breathing across the body. This will help to mentally zero yourself back into the moment, while biologically increasing blood oxygen levels to actively reduce blood pressure, pulse, and levels of adrenaline and cortisol (the stress hormones). By this point, your mind might have stopped grasping at an un-grabbable golden snitch and may be clear and objective enough to figure out something productive to do next!

42. Notice, right now, your focus of attention. What occupies your primary focus? How about the more subconscious secondary or tertiary processes?

As you observe yourself in this moment, try to notice as many things as possible, that you have been doing simultaneously on autopilot mode. Now that you are aware of some of these things you are doing, identify them individually:

I am breathing
I am sitting
I am looking
I am listening
I am hearing...

When we feel happy, we can appreciate the feeling on a deeper level, allowing gratefulness for the moment of happiness, multiplying its impact. If we identify undesired feelings, we can acknowledge them in the mix of the other present moment elements, and can process them far more healthily. This empowers us to choose where we focus our attention and hence choose to feel the feelings we want to experience more regularly or deeply.

43. How is it that one child is happy to play with a stick and a ball, wanting for nothing, while another child is frustrated by her iPad not having enough games? How are so many people with almost no material possessions, happier than so many others that own so much? Could understanding the psychological mechanics of this paradox enable us to become happier, whatever our social demographic may be? The answer may lie in "**Learned Contentment**".

Contentment often gets devalued in our busy lives, but oftentimes, a moment of contentment is exactly what we need, to achieve what we truly desire.

Contentment doesn't mean that achievements are unimportant. Well invested effort pays back far more as a valuable sense of meaningful contribution and growth, which fill the left half of the brain with a logical and value-aligned sense of happiness. However, it is also important to balance this goal orientation with the time to appreciate our contentment in the present moment, within the right hemisphere of the brain and the parietal lobe.

It is not all about the destination, the journey itself is where the magic happens! If you are sitting down at the end of a long day, taking off the work clothes and putting the disguise away for another day, or undoing that restrictive clothing and falling into the couch with a cup of tea; or if you are appreciating the present moment and all its sensory joys, the magic of touch, the subtleness of breath, the reassurance of gravity, the rich soundscape of life, the glorious sedation of digestion; you are practising the powerful happiness catalyst of contentment. Contentment is the appreciation of what we do have, right now, in the whole and truthful present moment.

And if you think contented happiness and high motivation towards great achievements is incompatible, keep reading this book!

44. We have seen that contentment is an ingredient of sustainable happiness that allows happiness to last and endure. Yet contentment without growth is a falsified and ephemeral contentment. It is the element of growth that differentiates real contentment from stagnant hedonistic self-indulgence.

We can therefore only unlock this genuine and sustainable contentment, by continually developing and constantly growing some aspect of our lives that is meaningful and of personal value or importance, if we are to truly enjoy it. This requires dedicated work.

Anne Frank delicately penned these words into her diary, when she wrote:

"Laziness may appear attractive, but
work gives satisfaction."

45. You know that feeling you get when you find some money hiding under the sofa cushions or in an old pair of jeans? That sense of victorious joy? Well, we can revive that sense of

elation more regularly than just the times we happen upon good fortune, and it doesn't involve hiding money in old pockets! When more common, less surprisingly profitable events happen, like when the sun comes up, or when your body performs as you would like it to; encourage yourself to revive those feelings of mini-victory, of pleased surprise, of grateful elation.

The unnoticed trivialities in life very quickly become far more useful. The less obviously profitable events become far more obviously profitable, and the days become filled with little good mood bursts that slowly merge together in a string of notes in a daily melody of joy.

There is always *something* we can feel good about if we practise opening our eyes properly!

46. What was the highlight of your day today? What was the best part of your last meal? What is the most relaxed part of your body right now? These kinds of questions help us to savour, and magnify the enjoyable aspects of the present moment, so we can find "even more" happiness right now. Savouring can be a short three-minute reflection on happy memories of the recent or more distant past, or you could ask these kinds of savouring questions to loved ones and see where the conversation leads.

Just remember that it is an exercise for savouring, not dwelling on the past with a craving to return to it or change it. When we explore the infinite reasons to feel happy in the present moment, without craving for anything to be different, we can be truly happy.

47. A 2013 study[4] from Brown University has highlighted strong evidence that the MBSR techniques (Mindfulness Based Stress Reduction) of increasing attention control have measurable effects on alpha wave behaviour in patients' brains. Alpha rhythms are a key part of the sensory system, and relate to how the brain processes and filters irrelevant sensory inputs. Filtering inputs is a crucial part of higher order cognitive process such as selective attention and working memory, which are based on a person's ability to focus on relevant information while ignoring irrelevant information. Without proper filtering, even the most basic cognitive operations can be crippled.

MBSR was also shown to have positive emotional benefits in those suffering from chronic pain and depression. It was reported that practitioners found greater happiness by densifying the grey matter around the amygdala; which is a part of the limbic system in the brain known to be important for emotion, especially feelings of stress, fear and anger. This resulted in reduced reactivity to negative stimuli and improved voluntary control over these emotional responses.

48. You have a human body! It is RIGHT THERE too. Always conveniently close by, it is operated by some magical telekinesis, just think a thought and a limb starts moving all by itself!

If NASA said they had developed a self-healing, telekinetically powered miracle machine that can teach itself new information and abilities, requires no electricity or fossil fuels, able to grow and adapt to almost any environment, able to feel joy and love and euphoria and tranquility, and then they said: YOU have exclusive control of it?!

This wonderful gift is more advanced than mankind's best technology, having taken millions of years to develop the complex design to this latest and most refined model. And it is completely and entirely yours! Free to use as you please. No strings attached! It might be time to take it for a little test drive and see what wonderful things it can do for you.

Hello! Did you know that with practice as happiness skills increase emotional intelligence also improves? That means we can learn to process emotions more healthily, understand how to deal with our own feelings better, and can make more meaningful connections with others. Increased "happiness intelligence" impacts many other social factors such as higher chances of marriage, lower divorce rates and stronger social networks. A recent study[5] revealed that people who rated themselves as happier than the average were also more philanthropic, volunteering more of their time and donating more money to charities.

Part Two:

The Lifestyle Steps

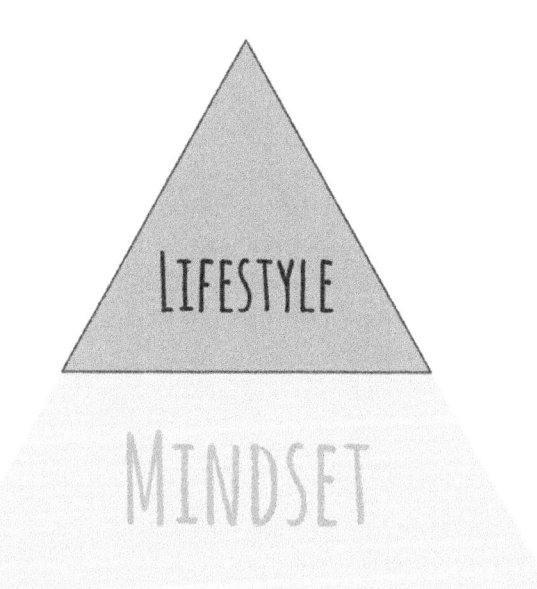

Part One of this guidebook has shown us that happiness is created and experienced in the mind, and we have learned how a gratitude-oriented mindset can be fed with positive thoughts in the present moment, to generate increased happiness.

From here we can grow *even more* happiness upon this foundation by creating a lifestyle that makes those mindset elements *even easier* and even more prevalent.

The objective of the following Lifestyle Steps is to facilitate greater happiness by acting as a catalyst for the mindset pieces. That is done by simplifying the process of realistic positive thinking, encouraging a mindful and present time perspective, and ultimately, by accommodating ever more reasons to feel grateful.

In the field of Positive Psychology, the lifestyle actions and activities that most influence our happiness are grouped in five major themes: Pleasure, Engagement (absorption of an enjoyed yet challenging activity), Relationships, Meaning (a perceived belonging to something bigger), and Accomplishments (realising tangible goals). These are also known as the "PERMA" model.

These lifestyle themes are most supportive of happiness when they are balanced and void of excess. Imbalances can manifest as anything from pleasure-seeking at the expense of meaningful relationships, to attaching one's sense of identity with one's accomplishments.

Some of the actions we take are naturally oriented around prioritising ourselves, such as our achievements, mentally engaging tasks, sources of pleasure and things like our physical and mental health. Others elements of our lifestyle choices are more connected with a wider environment, like our loving relationships and a sense of meaningful contribution toward something greater than just one isolated human life.

These are the two general orientations for the actions we take in our lives that impact our happiness. Some are more internally oriented, others more externally oriented. Like the two wings of a bird, or the wheels of a cart, they must be balanced in equal size and strength. If we focus only on our personal needs and neglect those around us, we may start to veer off course. Likewise, making serial personal sacrifices for the benefit of others can be equally unsustainable in the long run. This gives us the last two pieces of the puzzle:

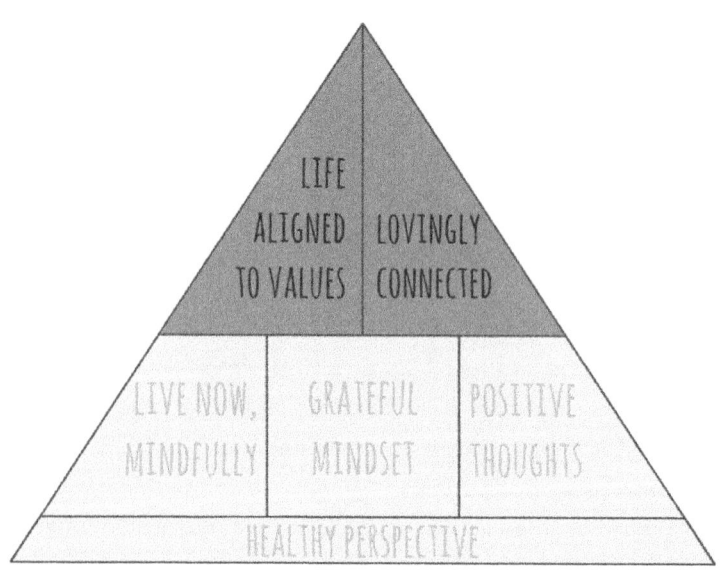

Balancing the actions we take for ourselves with our external interactions to build a life we can sustainably enjoy.

These elements represent the decisions we make throughout every day, they go side by side, as both types of action need to be balanced. The route to ultimate happiness, as Gautama the Buddha taught, is a balanced middle path. Certainly looking after personal needs and pleasurable activities is very important, and when combined with genuine compassion, the deeper feelings of genuine happiness are allowed to flourish through.

Let's first cover some of the steps to align our actions with the things that matter to us. Then we can look at building meaningful and loving connections with others.

Hi there! How is your mindfulness practice coming along? There are two main ways to practise mindfulness:

1. Informal Mindfulness — Paying attention, on purpose and non-judgmentally, to the present moment, as one goes about one's life. It is the practice of observing your body and mind, thoughts and feelings, as though from a distance, without any attachment, or trying to suppress or deny them.

2. Formal Mindfulness Meditation — Being still for a moment to observe the breath or the thoughts or the information from the sense doors that exist in this present moment. When concentration inevitably drifts to the future or past, patiently keep bringing the attention back to the sensations of the present moment.

A LIFE ALIGNED TO YOUR VALUES

49. To be happy we have to take the time to understand what we value most. Too few people seem to actually pause to consider what has true value for them. Too many people have spent great effort and sometimes made great sacrifices for values that, fundamentally, meet no meaningful needs for them personally. We can be subjected to misleading expectations from friends, family, colleagues or community, and to arrive at a clear understanding of one's own personal values can be difficult to achieve. However, to fail to "know thyself" is to leave the greatest happiness just out of reach.

   Taking the time to check in on yourself now and then, to reflect on the general direction of the various parts of your life in relation to how you deep down would like them to be going, is an important process indeed. Living a life that is enjoyable and meaningful to ourselves is the whole point of what life is for. The "Future Self" exercise is a nice little tool to get some idea of what a successfully happy life might look like to you as a unique individual.

   Close your eyes in a quiet place and imagine yourself celebrating your 100th birthday, looking back over your life, grateful for all those things you did, and imagine your future self, giving some words of advice to your "present-day self". What would you be saying about the things you are most proud of? What advice would the future you give the present day you about the things they regret the most? Words of wisdom? Comfort? Courage?

50. As we saw in Step 25, we can find great pleasure in the progression of some element of our lives. This pleasure can come from accomplishment related dopamine which is what computer game developers take advantage of to develop a dopamine addiction to their constantly progressing game-play. This can indicate the difference between pleasure and happiness. Pleasure may be short lasting and often involves dopamine, Happiness requires an additional ingredient: *Meaning.*

We can be so frequently comforted by the sense of progression coming from various parts of our lives, that we neglect the things that connect with our deepest sense of meaning. The excitement of the next promotion, the next big purchase, the very tangible progress of the next mortgage or finance repayment, the next qualification. These can all provide pleasure, but if they are something we value deeply, it becomes meaningful.

Progress without meaning, steals happiness for pleasure. So instead of focusing on blind progression, consider these questions to start thinking about your deepest personal values and turn pleasure back into happiness. You might want to write them down, or head over to the Happiness Archives at AGoodWayToThink.com to download the awesome full "Identifying Your Values" worksheet:

1. *If you could imagine a perfect day in your life, what would it look like?*
2. *What are five experiences in your life that you feel proud of?*
3. *What five things are you willing to die for?*
4. *What five character qualities do you find most admirable in other people?*

5. Over the course of your life, what are five experiences you have had, that made you feel truly alive?
6. Which five words describe you when you are at your best?
7. 200 years from today, what one thing do you want people to say about you?

51. Persistence is a great trait, but all the perseverance in the world is useless if we use the wrong methods.

When we hear the phrase "*You can achieve anything if you put your mind to it*", we accept we must also follow some universal laws of physics. Humans may fly, but only with the help of well thought out technology. To achieve anything, you must "...**put your mind to it**."

To this end, Jimmy Dean explained, "*I can't change the direction of the wind, but I can adjust my sails to always reach my destination.*"

We have achieved amazing things by combining imagination with technology, and a degree of hard work and perseverance. Whatever your challenge is, working hard is just the engine. Now and then we need to adjust our methods to navigate the right course. Being open minded to the advice of trusted loved ones can shed new insight into approaching situations, likewise, services like counselling and life-coaching can empower us to overcome negative or positive challenges respectively.

52. Intuition. A hunch. Gut instinct... Whatever you call it, it usually offers good advice to our true values at heart.

The more we practise following this intuition, listening to gut feelings, the more aware we become of the subtle messages our body and subconscious mind are suggesting.

Sometimes they whisper very quietly, so practising mindfulness can help tune into the subtler messages. The more we try to listen, the clearer the guidance becomes and the more easily we can live a life with a sense of meaning and purpose. So when you feel you have a hunch to do something: try to act on it. Each time you notice a thought of inspiration awakening your soul: feed it with attention and curiosity! At the very least, write it down somewhere you will revisit later, a "To Do list" of inspiring thoughts, just try not to let the intuition be lost before it has a chance to air.

Listening to these intuitive feelings allows the mystical inspiration delivery channel to open up, in turn permitting more inspiration to flow and guide us to a life that is meaningful to our unique personal values. Intuition is our unerring guide that we too often ignore from fear. It is each person's unique internal tutor that truly has their best interest at heart.

53. It is healthy to look forwards with focus and optimism, and as with all journeys, it is a good idea to keep an eye on where we want to go to ensure we are actually heading toward it!

We can benefit greatly by having a routine of checking in on ourselves every now and then, and New Year Resolutions may not be frequent enough. These checks ensure we are aware of the big picture things: the value of impermanent things; how well our time is prioritised among the things we love most; and that our thoughts and actions are aligned to our most important personal values, not just the values imposed on us by society.

Do you have a written record of your personal values? Or which changes within your life would keep you aligned to these values as the environment around you constantly transforms.

As long as time is passing, we are heading somewhere via our constant decisions and indecisions. Better to make sure we're heading somewhere we want to go.

54. Having fun and enjoying yourself is important! People that responded to a survey saying they enjoy silliness, were also 33% more likely to say they feel happy.

Having fun isn't about forcing ourselves to do what other people like to do, and nor is it about trying to do things we feel we probably *should* find fun. Happiness is not simply the removal of sadness, it is a positive, energising magical thing that we can experience and enjoy by letting go of restricting inhibitions, destructing fears, and doing the activities that we personally find fun.

Fun may be only one of many ingredients for a happy life, but it can really make a huge difference very quickly.

Did you know that happier people are around half as likely to catch the cold virus and have a 50% lower risk of experiencing a cardiovascular event, such as a heart attack or stroke, than their less optimistic peers![20] They do say "Laughter is the best medicine"!

55. What were you doing when you last felt great? Was it seeing a friend, practising a hobby, getting out in nature, or some other activity that brings you a sense of joy? Being aware of what brings you joy is a super important first step, the next is to make sure it exists in your life! So check your calendar or diary today and see if you give yourself enough time to do the things that make you feel great.

Remember, you are in control of your calendar and your life via the decisions you make. We always have a choice.

And if you can bring in a deeper sense of meaning to the fun activity, then you've cracked a very special thing called happiness.

56. Wealth and riches don't bring happiness and creativity. Our creativity and happiness are what bring wealth and riches. So we cannot be really great at our work if our work is all we are. Instead of trying to earn what we want to earn, if we try to act how we want to feel, we bypass the entire trap of *pursuing* happiness and empower ourselves to create it directly.

   The more we practise anything the better we become at it, the same rule follows if we practise acting in a way we want to act. This can work for anything from trying to "under-react" to problems we may typically overreact to, or pretending to be enthusiastic, loving, and verbally grateful.

   Whichever well-thought-out improvements you may want to make to your typical mindset, ACTING how you want to *feel*, pretty quickly FEELS the more natural way of acting.

57. If you are ever questioning what you are doing with your life, (and it is a very good question to ask every now and then), just remember that EVERYONE is improvising! It is impossible for anyone, anywhere, ever, to know for certain which are ultimately the best decisions to make, so we all just figure things out as we go along.

   If it seems like everyone else has their lives figured out except you, or if you are worried about how to best navigate your career path, take a breath and remember that no-one knows anything for certain, everyone else is improvising too! People often like to present the image that they have cracked the puzzle of life, but we're all in this amazing improvising life-boat together.

So of course, ask the big questions, and keep thinking about the answers, just don't get caught up worrying about immediately finding all the "right" answers. Keep taking proactive steps in an ever-happier direction and you are bound to make sound progress.

58. The choices we make define who we are and how we are. Humans have a unique capacity to choose how we view the world, which builds our idea of who we are.

Which personality traits would you like to possess? Richness, health, selfishness, desire to impress, patience, desire to succeed, compassion?

Write them down somewhere you will see regularly.

Which personality traits do your lifestyle choices nurture and encourage? What traits surround you and what does your life bring out of you?

Keep the list of desired personality traits visible and prominent to let the words take root in your subconscious and help them grow naturally in you.

It is us that make our decisions, and it is our decisions that make us.

59. Exercise can really simplify the whole process of feeling happy! A quick ten-minute walk can increase our energy and boost our mood both in the short term and long term. Even micro-exercises such as standing up for 10 seconds while

reading an email can flush stress hormones, increase blood oxygen levels for better rational thinking, memory retrieval, creativity and problem solving, and makes us feel better!

People may say they're too tired to exercise, but unless we exercise at a very intense level, exercise typically boosts energy levels rather than depletes them. Serotonin is released during exercise, along with a wild cocktail of endorphins. These are released from the pituitary gland of the brain during periods of strenuous exercise, and help relieve pain and induce feelings of pleasure or euphoria, also attributed to the almost euphoric sensation of "Runner's High".

60. When people are having a good day, you'd be right in thinking they are less likely to feel the need to comfort eat with unhealthy snacks and fast food. And on those happier days, you'd also be right in guessing, since the comfort foods lose power against our heightened willpower, people typically eat more fruit and vegetables.

A dose-response relationship was shown in the largest study[6] into this phenomena to date, indicating the more portions of fruit and vegetables consumed per day, the higher the life satisfaction and happiness. This correlation was significant up to around 7 to 8 portions per day, and was evident after controlling for demographic and health factors such as employment status, income, education, major illnesses, exercise, smoking, and BMI.

One known contributing factor is due to the higher doses of vitamin C in fruit and vegetables, which is a co-factor in the production of dopamine.

Another study[7] took this relationship beyond happiness and showed that on the days in which more fruit and vegetables were consumed the participants also felt "more creative, curious, and a sense of greater eudaimonic well-being". Participants were flourishing.

But this all only confirms the comprehensive research already proving a happier mood leads to healthier food choices. Finally however, in 2013, a peer-reviewed study from the University of Otago in New Zealand[8], details a lagged analysis, concluding that "fruit and vegetable consumption predicted improvements in positive affect the next day, and not vice-versa".

Choosing healthier foods isn't simply the *result of* feeling happier on that day, but is also the *precursor to* feeling happier on the subsequent day also.

So if it's choosing an apple and orange over a packet of crisps, or a vegetable curry over a burger, knowing the impact of your diet on your happiness might just empower you to follow an even happier path than before.

61. D vitamins are produced in the skin during exposure to sunlight (and any other 280-320 nm wavelength lights). They are required for many natural bodily functions, including regulating the absorption of calcium and phosphorous (important for healthy bones), facilitating normal immune system function, and activating mood-related brain hormones serotonin and oxytocin.

Through the darker winter months between late October and early March, anyone further north than 40 degrees latitude (Madrid, New York, Beijing) receives such low-intensity UVB radiation that our skin cannot synthesise vitamin D. This is due to the low angle of sunlight being partially reflected by the earth's atmosphere.

Our bodies can store some amount of vitamin D from the sunnier months of summer, however, these reserves are often insufficient to meet our bodies natural vitamin D demands. For this reason, many people become susceptible to Seasonal Affective Disorder – a type of depression associated with prolonged lack of adequate UVB radiation from sunlight upon the skin.

Fortunately, we can meet our bodies natural vitamin D demands with a healthy balanced diet. Natural dietary sources of vitamin D include fish oils, egg yolk, tofu, fortified cereals, and fortified non-dairy milks. Using sunbeds is not a recommended way of making vitamin D, however, the British National Health Service does advise everyone over the age of five years to consider taking a daily supplement containing 10 micrograms (mcg) of vitamin D. This may not, however, be necessary through the summer months. They also advise speaking to your pharmacist, GP or health visitor if you are unsure whether you need to take a vitamin D supplement.

62. There's more to sunlight than just activating vitamin D production.

The spectrum of wavelengths in sunlight also stimulates the release of melatonin, which activates the hypothalamus – a part of the brain which helps regulate mood, appetite and sleep. Melatonin works with serotonin to improve our energy and alertness.

A groundbreaking 2014 study[9] has shown that UVA radiation from sunlight activates the release of nitric oxide, which relaxes the arteries and reduces blood pressure and the risks of heart disease, all while reducing damaging stress hormones, helping to regulate sleep, and increasing levels of serotonin!

Keeping your head up when walking outside and (whenever practical) being a sunflower to the sky might do us more good than we often think. Just keep in mind that overexposure to the Sun's rays can be extremely harmful to the skin and can lead to skin cancer. Heart disease is responsible for 40 times more deaths in the UK than skin cancers. In the US is it 60 times more.

Hey there, me again! Did you know that B vitamins (B6 in particular) support the production and function of serotonin, melatonin and dopamine in the brain? They're the multitalented chemicals that enable us to enjoy living a happy life! Check the glossary at the end of the book for more on what they do.

63. Changing routine pleasures can help reduce the vice of taking things for granted, and can even help train the mind for enhanced appreciation and gratitude – the seeds from which happiness grows!

Diversifying your diet is one option, or how about branching out into a wider social network, or scheduling in a weekly "Do something new (and fun) today" to help you find a novel source of joy.

By mixing up sources of pleasure they feel much more special, and the new experiences often lead to unexpected new benefits; from a wider social network to an undiscovered new favourite hobby!

64. Get dirty with the *Mycobacterium Vaccae*. There is a magical bacterium that thrives in soil, called Mycobacterium

Vaccae, which has been found to trigger the release of serotonin[10], which in turn elevates mood and decreases anxiety.

This microscopic hero has even been found to improve cognitive function[11] as well as many amazing health benefits that come with increased happiness, and is now showing strong potential to treat cancers and other diseases such as Crohn's disease and rheumatoid arthritis!

We can benefit from its uplifting effects by getting soil on the skin such as through gardening, playing outside or walking barefoot, and to a lesser extent through inhaling air near to freshly turned soil!

So why not get out there and get dirty with the world and see if reconnecting with this wonderful planet puts a smile on your soul too.

65. The phrase "No good deed goes unnoticed", may be down to our inherent biological reward system, governed by our ever-present moral compass.

What that means is that making the effort to do something selfless, for the benefit of others, such as volunteering some time to a worthy cause or achieving something meaningful towards a personal value, will almost always activate the subconscious dopamine reward systems in our brain and make us feel good.

Giving away something precious as an act of charity, be it your time or something more tangible, typically triggers a sense of meaningful contribution, a valuable element of the happiness mix. Sometimes good deeds yield contentment, other times joy, other times a deep and comforting sense of good-heartedness. Sometimes when our lives are filled with mind-cluttering thoughts, our awareness of these moral rewards can become reduced, and their effects appear to be more subtle. When we regain some degree of stillness to the mind, the subtleties become clearer, and simpler to acknowledge. Busy hectic schedules can make it harder to identify these moral rewards from wholesome actions.

On the other end of the "no good deeds go unnoticed" spectrum, is that all of the above is true for selfish, universally detrimental tasks. Instead of triggering dopamine and pleasant left prefrontal cortex activity, feelings of guilt, denial, elevated stress and self-loathing, activate the release of hormones such as cortisol and adrenalin, and unpleasant right prefrontal cortex activity. These hormones can accelerate the ageing process of our DNA and contribute to many other undesired effects on our health.

Some may try to ignore the function of their moral compass, justifying actions with greed, or resorting to mental distraction techniques such as occupying the mind with work, TV or the internet, however, these internal systems, are physiological systems. They are insuppressible, influencing us on a biochemical level.

Our ability to feel at ease with ourselves and our choices is a powerful factor in sustainable happiness.

66. A regular dose of some kind of novelty is a great way to continue learning and growing from new experiences, which can all deepen our understanding of happiness. We can benefit from creating this sense of novelty by changing up some of the long-standing routines in our lives, from things as

simple as rearranging the furniture, to redecorating, or joining a new social club, to making one friend every month.

The objective is to create a genuine sense of novelty into our lives, as this releases exciting dopamine whenever the mind is engaged in new and interesting tasks. This then acts as an uplifting motivational force to make other progressive changes within an atmosphere of growth.

Extreme levels of daily novelty and unpredictability, can potentially elevate levels of cortisol, especially if it comes with a lack of stability or any easily recognisable progression, however a healthy balance of routine novelty with progressive learning and understanding is a fantastic way to keep the day to day mind engaged and motivated, and can be a valuable source of meaningful progression.

"If you think adventure is dangerous, try routine; it is lethal." — Paulo Coelho.

67. Speaking of our decisions, these choices we make are the one unique thing that you have, that nobody else has any control over. That means you have control of how you live your life...the career path you choose, how positively you will interpret events, how you fill your day, which talents and skills you will nurture and so on.

Through these decisions, we are in control of – **and responsible for** – the majority of our happiness, the well-being of every sentient being that comes into contact with you, and by knock-on effect, the future of all life on the planet! Since our Happiness is emotionally contagious to the countless millions of people within three degrees of separation from you, you are literally the only person that can make *your personal impact*. What a great opportunity.

68. The '20-40-60 Rule' often helps dissolve many worries and stresses, especially reducing some pressure off any decisions you might be thinking about after the last few steps! It goes like this:

"At 20, we are constantly worrying about what other people think of us. At 40, we wake up and say 'I'm not going to give a damn what other people think of me anymore', and at 60, we realise that no one was really thinking about us all along!"

This rule is a light-hearted reminder that only *we* live our lives. Of course people love one another and care for each other, but in terms of making the decisions to live a life true to our values, no-one can possibly tell us exactly what is in our best interest as they simply do not know. People are preoccupied with trying to figure out what is best for themselves. We are responsible for our own fears and we are responsible for our own happiness. If fear of judgement is holding you back from living a life true to your values, have another read of the 20-40-60 rule.

Everyone inherently just wants to be happy themselves and free from suffering. We are all in this together!

69. When we build our sense of identity on things outside our control such as Titles, cars, money, looks, partners, etc.; we put our entire sense of personal identity at risk. These external things are impermanent, and will at some point change. When they do change, we are forced to confront and update our sense of identity, and our sense of self-worth. What is a footballer when she is forced to retire? What is a millionaire without her money?

We can build a resistance to this potential unhappiness by remembering that we are not defined by the things we temporarily own.

By instead defining ourselves by things within our control, such as the actions we take and how we take them, our sense of identity and self-worth can never be taken away. We can build an identity based on our individual experiences and the decisions we took through them.

Furthermore, when it comes to spending money on our happiness, experiences trump tangible items every time. Materials are far more comparable, so we may become upset if we later realise we could have had a better deal, or if we feel our item is trumped by someone else's.

70. How much does physical exercise impact our happiness? Aerobic exercise has been known for a long time to boost one's positive mood. In 2005, researchers at Chicago State University and the University of Minnesota analysed 158 different studies conducted between 1979 and 2005[12]. The effect of aerobic exercise was consistently positive and was especially noticeable when one started an exercise session while feeling a little more "down" than usual. In other words,

physical exercise was proven to have an uplifting impact on mood.

In a more recent paper[13] from Halmstad University in Sweden, researchers analysed 15 different studies and found that physical exercise consistently worked as an effective treatment for mild and moderate depression.

The body and the mind are coupled far more than we often think – a couple of minutes of jumping jacks might just help you change the world!

71. We saw in Part One that positive thoughts and positive emotions are a key foundation to sustainable happiness. Feeling truly alive, with endorphins coursing through the veins certainly fits into this category!

Whatever morally safe activity you can do, perhaps something you have done in the past that gave some rush of vivacious zeal, accommodate it into your life as often as practicable! Some pour their hearts into snowsports and water-sports, though that may not do it for you. For others, the great zest of life comes from wild adventures, running in the rain purely for the sake of getting wet, or standing upon a mountain filled with accomplishment and self-respect, but that may not be right for you either. Perhaps you are most thrilled by the rush that comes with being vulnerable to judgement, performing arts or leaping outside your social comfort zone?

Whatever you do that offers that beautiful realisation that you are alive; truly alive, feeds the faculty of happiness tremendously. When combined with an awareness of these feelings (the "Live Now, Mindfully" element), these activities can trigger meaningful and lasting boosts to mood and emotional well-being. When further combined with the "Grateful Mindset" element, we can multiply the impact of the positive emotions and achieve a lasting uptick in overall life satisfaction.

Noticing that you have cultivated a happiness-multiplying mindset can then offer a new reason to be grateful. This is the remarkable process of compound happiness whereby being aware of one's gratefulness generates additional gratitude, and its byproduct: happiness; and in turn restarts the cycle.

When we feel alive, we are happy; when we feel happy, we are truly alive!

72. Fear greatly impedes happiness, but on the other side of that coin, happiness greatly impedes fear!

Investing time and effort into understanding, embracing, and prioritising our happiness means we can make decisions based on happiness, compassion and love, as opposed to decisions from fear and ignorance; which unlocks the best life we can possibly live and helps everyone we connect with too.

The noblest way to live is by endeavouring to bring happiness to others. That can be achieved in any number of ways, such as the traditional methods of teaching, peacekeeping, raising a good family or leading by inspirational example. Another, universally available solution, that doesn't require a career change or starting a family, is also the best way to make others happy, is to **be happy yourself!**

Among many other benefits, happiness in people is infectious! Happier people are more productive, healthier, and significantly more altruistic. So if the first ingredient to a good life for all is to be happy oneself, then focusing on your happiness cannot be selfish. Neither is it self-sacrificial – prioritising one's happiness is *universally beneficial*. Once we truly understand our own happiness, we automatically live an honest, noble and infectiously uplifting life.

So what is the best way to be happy yourself? The next few steps may give you some clues!

LOVING CONNECTIONS WITH OTHERS

73. Positive social connections are a cornerstone of happiness and health. A conversation with a friend can have a lasting positive effect, increasing our energy and cultivating  greater motivation for action. Simply belonging to a social group involving some degree of emotional connection with another

 person has been shown to create a significant and lasting increase in health and happiness.

So if there are people in your life that you appreciate, however close or distant you feel, get in touch with them and say hi! Maybe there is someone around you right now as you are reading this? In the name of health and happiness get a little closer and help make the world a better place!

74. To be happy we must have reason to be happy. It must be pure reason – our subconscious cannot be tricked! We cannot bribe our minds to be deeply happy with wealth and fortune if we know it was obtained through immoral and selfish means. We can only enjoy complete happiness when there is no guilt attached to it. When our happiness is obtained with

no detriment to others, but instead developed sustainably, by providing happiness to others.

"If you want others to be happy, practise compassion. If you want to be happy, practise compassion."
— 14th Dalai Lama

Peaceful happiness must come from a selfless objective. It is a bit like money and health, you can enjoy it the most when it is shared equally among everybody. Buddhist teachings often emphasise the immense value of total universal compassion for the benefit of all, especially the subject practising it. Selfishness and ego destroy happiness, altruism and compassion fertilise it. While it is worth investing time and effort into our fellow humans, we can go a step further and develop compassion for all sentient beings to enhance our ability to love and feel loved.

Hey you there! The next time you see a "YOU ARE HERE" sign, pause your life for just a moment to think about what that really means.

Until then, let's balance the focus of our lifestyle actions with some steps less about us and more about nurturing meaningful connections with others.

75. Let's continue the momentum of that step with this excellent meditation based on building a sense of loving kindness and wishes of wellbeing for all.

Start by sitting in a comfortable and relaxed position, and take two or three deep breaths with slow, long and complete exhalations, then breathe naturally. Next, place your attention on the area in the middle of your chest, around your heart and quietly, mentally repeat, slowly and steadily, the following (or similar phrases):

May I be well.
May I be peaceful.
May I be loved.
May my heart be filled with love.
May I be happy.

While you say these phrases, keeping your focus on the core of the body, try to notice feelings of pleasant sensations and allow yourself to enjoy the experience of filling your body with love. Allow yourself to sink into the intentions the phrases express.

After a short period of directing loving-kindness toward yourself, bring into your mind someone you love and respect. Then slowly repeat phrases of loving-kindness toward them:

May you be well.
May you enjoy peace, and harmony.
May you feel loved.
May you be happy.

Next, bring to mind someone else you like and respect, and send them these feelings of warmth and compassion with the above phrases or others similar. As you continue the meditation, you can bring to mind other friends, neighbours, acquaintances, strangers, animals, and finally people with whom you have difficulty. Perhaps someone you got irritated with recently, or if you wish, someone who has hurt you in the past. You might not want to do this early in your practice of loving-kindness. If feelings such as anger, grief, or sadness arise, remember that there is no need to judge yourself for having these feelings. Take these as signs that your heart is softening.

You may want to work towards including someone you carry bitterness, hatred or resentment towards, remembering also that you are not condoning or approving their actions, simply allowing yourself to let go of any pain or ill-will you carry towards them. This pain and anger only hurts you. Replacing it with feelings of love and compassion will be like applying a soothing balm on any emotional wounds, and results in your own peace, your own heart being filled with love, and ultimately your genuine happiness.

Radiate the warmth and love to all the beings around you, and finally, return the attention to yourself. Return to the sensations through the core of the body, and the air flowing into your lungs. Return to your body and the rich soundscape in which you sit, and open your eyes.

76. Who has been great to you recently? Take a second to think of your answer!

Visualise this person. What do they mean to you? What did they do that was great? What might they have been thinking when they were "being great" to you? Take a moment to answer these questions.

And how do you feel about that person now?

The questions we ask ourselves can make a huge a difference in how we think, act and feel. Taking a moment now and then to ask yourself who else has been great to you recently, can bring new warmth and light into the day and the relationships we have. If you are grateful to have someone as a meaningful connection, they'd probably love to hear about the impact they made!

77. What you do **to** others, you do **to** yourself. What you do **for** others, you do **for** yourself.

Whatever you account this cause and effect relationship to, whether you thank karma or fate, a godly cosmic coordinator or research from the scientific community, our actions arise from thoughts, which arise from emotions. We physiologically must imagine (and experience) an emotion before we can act to distribute it to others. Be it love or neglect, we feel it before we output it.

Try doing someone a favour, a small act of generosity a gesture of kindness, and see if this statement holds true. What do you feel immediately before taking the action?

What you do to others, you do to yourself. What you do for others, you do for yourself, so to FEEL GOOD, BE GOOD, DO GOOD!

The pleasant endorphins the subconscious mind releases when we perform noble acts also help reduce stress and improve our cognitive functions as well as boosting our physical health so tune into this subtle reward system and align your actions to it!

In one study[14], 255 medical students took a personality test designed to assess their level of hostility. Twenty-five years later, it was found that the most aggressive among them had suffered five times more cardiac events than those who were less irritable.

78. Allow yourself to feel great by getting in touch with an uplifting friend... Right now! We get a huge boost from connecting with other people, especially if they are emotionally meaningful to us such as old friends or family, and also if they are positive and uplifting characters themselves. Don't be afraid of reaching out, whether you feel in need of a happiness boost and its phenomenal benefits, or you just enjoy living a happy life, reaching out to people we care about is super simple and super effective, for introverts and extroverts alike.

79. An extensive study[15] in the British Medical Journal monitored people over twenty years and found that their happiness levels affected other people in their networks across "three degrees of separation". In other words, how happy we are has a measurable impact on the mood of our friend's friend's friends!

The study concluded *"Clusters of happy and unhappy people are visible in the network, and the relationship between people's happiness extends up to three degrees of separation. People who are surrounded by many happy people and those who are central in the network are more likely to become happy in the future.*

Longitudinal statistical models suggest that clusters of happiness result from the spread of happiness and not just a tendency for people to associate with similar individuals. A person who becomes happy increases the probability that a friend who lives within a mile (about 1.6 km) is happy, by 25% The effect decays with time and with geographical separation."

This is congruent with research at Harvard University[16], which looked at smoking cigarettes and also found that *"although a person may be connected to other people by six degrees of separation, he or she is influenced only by those up to three degrees away."*

This demonstrates the importance of maintaining positively nourishing social connections, and minimising long-term exposure to personalities that make an overall negative impact on one's happiness.

80. It is often the efforts we put into our achievements that become more valuable and rewarding than obtaining the end goal itself. Take this beautiful quote from Albert Einstein:

> "A human being is a part of the whole, called
> by us, Universe, a part limited in time and
> space. He experiences himself, his thoughts and
> feeling as something separated from the rest, a
> kind of optical delusion of his consciousness. This
> delusion is a kind of prison for us, restricting us to
> our personal desires and to affection for a few
> persons nearest to us. Our task must be to free
> ourselves from this prison by widening our circle
> of compassion to embrace all living creatures
> and the whole of nature in its beauty."

It can sometimes be hard to follow good advice, even when it comes a world renowned genius like Albert here, but it is important to remember that it is the act of striving for such an achievement, that is in itself, the most valuable element, the most influential ingredient for our adventure of life.

81. Only when we try to do good deeds without expectation of remuneration – without the action being motivated by hope for some future payback – only then does karma work. Karma isn't necessarily just a spiritual phenomenon either, neurological and physiological reactions have been observed in brain scans indicating that when we perform noble tasks such as caring for others, the mind activates reward systems in the brain and releases dopamine and oxytocin, which

biologically give feelings of joy and pleasure from doing good actions. This is physiological mechanics behind the "no good deed goes unnoticed" idea of Step 65.

So let's take this to the next level by playing *The Karma Game* today! It may seem counter-intuitive at first, but just see what happens if you challenge yourself to perform some anonymous acts of kindness! To help others without allowing anyone to know it was provided by you.

82. Humans are social beings — we thrive on physical human contact, from a handshake with eye contact to a close hug, the feeling of physical connection releases endorphins and oxytocin — the trust and attachment specialist chemical nicknamed the "Love Hormone" — into the bloodstream. This biological reaction strengthens relationships tremendously and is responsible for our sense of connectedness to something more than just ourselves. This sense of connectedness is an important component of happiness and we have the power to positively impact it by choosing to connect more through physical contact.

Every other mammal, from cats and dogs to troops of wild monkeys and dolphins, they all use the connection boosting power of physical contact to build and maintain relationships. It is healthy to live how we have evolved to be.

83. Take this to the next level and hug for your happiness! Physical contact is a vital relationship building connectedness

generating tool, but we can do much more than shaking hands, holding hands and the occasional high five. It has recently been shown that after hugging for around 6 – 10 seconds, our brains start to release serotonin (the multi-talented neurotransmitter and mood improving hormone), melatonin (the appetite and sleep-regulating hormone) and you may have guessed it, great swathes of oxytocin. These predominant *happiness hormones* are generally influential over, if not responsible for, our feelings of happiness, connectedness and being emotionally comforted.

These neurological systems have been replicated when hugging teddy bears and blankets, as well as pets, friends or life partners, so whoever you hug, whenever you hug them, hug sincerely and enthusiastically for the sake of your happiness!

84. Can we help our environment to help us feel happy? We sure can! Nurturing "Happiness Catalysts" all around us is one of the best ways.

A good social network isn't based on competition for the appearance of popularity or success, which inadvertently encourages a reliance on validation or praise; instead, when our relationships are built on compassion, with trust and meaning, the people around us become our magical "*Happiness Catalysts*". They are the people that can make the world shine with genuine reasons to feel happy. Friends, family and other amazing souls can all brighten up our mood totally out of the blue when it is least expected, sometimes stimulating a memory to be grateful of or providing solace and support in times of need.

Can you be a Happiness Catalyst for someone else today? Compassion is truly a boomerang. It might fly away and take a course of its own, but the love you put out into the world, will come back with astonishing accuracy!

85. "*Spontaneous Trait Transference*" is a psychological term for an interesting phenomenon that occurs when we describe somebody to other people. It has been shown[17] that the traits we describe in others, also become associated with us as the storyteller, by the conversation partners. That is to say that if we tell a friend that a colleague is very compassionate, the friend associates the trait of compassion with us, as well as the described colleague.

Whether we describe others as loving or arrogant, conscientious or selfish, we may be subconsciously influencing people's opinions of ourselves, impacting their present moment comfort, as well as the longer-term relationship. Many of the steps in Part One can help brighten conversations toward more nourishing uplifting subjects. This becomes additionally important when we understand the next step, Emotional Contagion, below.

86. "Smile and the whole world smiles with you!" Well perhaps not the WHOLE world smiles with you, but hyperbole aside, this ripple effect of happiness is attributed to the universal psychological trait of **_Emotional Contagion_**[18]. Our subconscious minds pick up on the expressions, vocalizations, postures and movements of another person, and empathises with them to such a degree that it replicates the associated hormones with the perceived emotional state. What that means is our minds synthesise the feelings we see in others.

So smile and the world really might smile back.

Hi again, I hope you're having a GREAT day! Did you know that it was Positive Psychology researcher Sonja Lyubomirsky who coined the popularly accepted definition of happiness as "The experience of joy, contentment, or positive well-being, combined with a sense that one's life is good, meaningful, and worthwhile." So it is this combination of generally happier present moment emotions, (regularly feeling grateful or joyous without too many "negative emotions"), combined with the broader feeling that one's life is worth something according to your personal values.

ACTION AND RESPONSIBILITY

We are conditioned through our developmental years to follow the instructions of other people, parents, education systems and the wider society in general. We are told what we can and cannot touch, what we can and cannot eat, what to learn, which books to read, homework to do, clothes to wear... we are quite comprehensively, instructed how to live. While many of these lessons are absolutely in our best interests, such an environment can breed complacency to further learning how to live a harmonious and happy life. The assumption may develop that we have been completely taught how to live, and we may become unaccustomed to, or even averse to self-directed learning and betterment. When the support system inevitably reduces as we transition toward more autonomous adulthood, a fundamental attitude of personal responsibility must be adopted.

This responsibility cannot be transferred to anyone else — it is up to us to live our lives, to take the steps, to apply the advice, to take the risks, to feel the vulnerability and to implement the changes. No-one else can undertake this journey, and however far you progress, it is a journey you will not regret taking.

Most happiness increasing techniques are easy to learn and understand, but far harder to implement on a consistent basis. Like New Year's Resolutions, the key is determination and consistency.

Only through consistent training and practice can anyone achieve greatness, be that physical ability, academic intellect, musical talent, spiritual peace or sustainable contented happiness. The more time and effort invested, the greater the results. Knowledge is useless until it is applied.

So far in this book we have dissected the different elements of our lives that can influence our happiness, including ways of thinking and ways of acting. Now need to bring it all together.

Here are the parts so far:

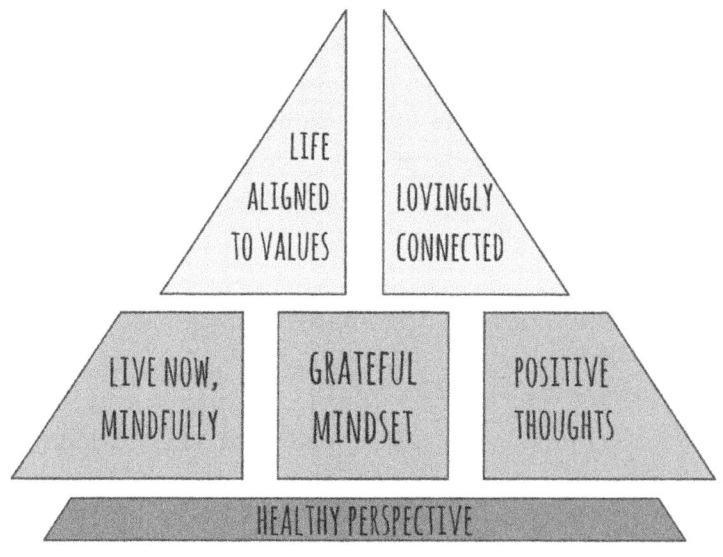

The major ingredients of sustainable and sincere happiness.

In order to pull this all together and give it a sense of unified resilience, we need one more thing. This final element epitomises the dichotomy between looking at a journey on a map, and physically experiencing the path. This is what takes our exercises and ideas and turns them into a driving force that brings tangible results. This is the uniting effect of taking responsibility, ownership and action.

87. The way we act influences the way we feel. It has been shown that when people move faster and more energetically, their metabolism speeds up. What that means is that when we pretend to have lots of energy, it genuinely makes us feel more energetic. Anything from standing up while talking on the phone, to walking just a little quicker, from raising your eyebrows just a little higher and speaking with more animation, to simply making your legs jump under the desk. **Pretending** to have more energy, **GIVES** more energy!

Similarly pretending to be lovingly and compassionate makes us feel more loving and compassionate, and acting joyfully produces feelings of further joy!

88. Wanting to be happier is a valuable first step, however, it is only a first step. It is the same as wanting to learn a new skill like a musical instrument, first having the desire is absolutely necessary before mastery of it. And just like with learning any other skill, the desire isn't enough. There is more we have to do than just want to be better at something: we have to devote time and effort to the cause as well. Reading a book about swimming won't teach anyone how to swim.

With access to so much information in the world, it is easy to become a tourist of information, visiting the knowledge centres and taking an observational understanding of the subject. But this information tourism changes nothing. Reading the menu of a restaurant doesn't cure our hunger just as discussing the active ingredients of a medicine doesn't cure the ailment. The food must be eaten, the medicine must be ingested, and the swimming lesson might get you a bit wet, but that's just the way it is!

We have to practise and practise some more, learn and apply. If *great* achievements were easy, everyone would be doing them and they would become *normal* achievements. Musicians aren't born able to play musical instruments; athletes aren't born ready to run a marathon or work the parallel bars; doctors stay in education for so many years for a reason; carpenters require apprenticeships to learn the skills to do the job; academics spend their lives learning because the knowledge is complex and takes time to master. This, we all seem to accept...

Yet when it comes to happiness, it is so often assumed that we can just choose to be happier. That we can simply, "Look on the bright side of life" and miraculously rewire generations of neural evolution; immediately developing the synapses and thought habits to be grateful and positive and aware of every sense in this present moment. That we can densify the grey matter around the amygdala overnight, to enable us to better regulate our mood through any emotional turmoil, and that we can voluntarily increase the serotonin and dopamine production systems within the brain. All this by simply *wanting* to be happier?

Humans *can* learn to play the violin, we *can* learn mathematics, medicine and masonry. We can train ourselves to run marathons and do the splits. Most people with skills feel accomplished and proud that they invested their time and efforts into themselves, to achieve what they have achieved. Graduates celebrate graduation for a reason!

So it is truly wonderful and absolutely imperative that people **want** to be *even happier* in order to **be** *even happier*. The volition is the first step of a very wonderful path: the warm up, the introduction, grade 1. There are such beautiful rewards on every single step of this journey.

89. A great way to motivate ourselves to achieve some desired change is to replace the concept of "Goals" with one of "Resolutions". We hit a goal, but we pledge to keep a resolution.

Too difficult goals become discouraging and demotivating, too easy and we either stop trying once the goal is accomplished or it never motivated us to try in the first place. Even when a good goal is completed we feel that familiar "now what?"

With resolutions, every day is an opportunity to succeed, and we are less discouraged when they're challenging because no day is a failure, each day is an opportunity to learn, improve, and grow.

Keeping resolutions has also been shown to be significantly more effective when each resolution is monitored by some visual type of performance tracking system, such as putting ticks on every successful day on your calendar or a resolution chart.

This helps nurture an important and highly motivating *Atmosphere of Growth*, so don't be afraid of targeting an area of big potential improvement. It's also best to be specific with resolutions, so instead of a mental note to "Go to bed on time," track your performance to a pledge: "I will have all lights out by 10:00 pm, five nights per week!"

Finally, reviewing your resolutions every month helps keep them fresh and relevant. Head over to AGoodWayToThink.com/Happiness-Archives to download your own free Resolution Chart.

90. Have you ever noticed yourself thinking; *"It would be so lovely if someone did x,y,z for me..."* Well, the chances are that someone else somewhere has thought that too!

You could be that "someone!"

Imagine that other person's delight resulting from your acts of loving kindness... their glee and gratitude at finding a pre-paid parking ticket, or a nice anonymous thank you note, a door being held open or coming home to a clean house, a bouquet of flowers, or a cooked meal. You can be the someone making someone else feel great!

Acts of random kindness are as contagious as laughter, and provided you don't *expect* it to, that lovely happiness will come back to you faster than you can possibly give it out.

91. Not only is the purpose of our lives to be happy, not only is it our right to be happy, it is our duty to live harmoniously with the happiness of all, only then can we truly experience

happiness. True happiness must be shared. As John Hossack said: "*No man is free until all men are free*". Even micro-progress like taking three conscious breaths, decluttering a living or working space, or turning off distracting electronic devices is a start.

92. Scientists estimate if we cured cancer tomorrow, we would add between 3 — 4 years on average life expectancies for men and women in the developed world. Research from Yale University[19] identified a repeatable extension of average life expectancy of around 7.5 years for people that were more positive and happy!

    Heart disease is an even bigger story and is by a large margin the number one cause of death in most developed countries such as the UK and US. A 2012 US study from Harvard[20] identified that "the most optimistic individuals had an approximately 50% reduced risk of experiencing an initial cardiovascular event compared to their less optimistic peers."

    So while the scientific communities work on cures for cancers, let's fight back with a smile, some positive thinking and living with joy and happiness too

93. Contemporary research has now shown that when we train the brain in happiness enhancing exercises like the steps in this guidebook, it becomes more productive[2, 21, 22], more compassionate[23] and altruistic[24], more socially likeable[25], more creative[2], significantly healthier[26, 27], and many more tremendous benefits!! Beyond a better brain, happier people

also build more rewarding relationships as we become more collaborative[2] within a more conscientious society.

Possibly trumping all the science is the fact that we *feel better* when we feel better! Prioritising happiness is not only good for us, it is vital for us and every living thing in this beautiful world!

Epicurus wrote of its fundamental integrity to our lives:

> "We must exercise ourselves in the things which
> bring happiness, since, if that be present, we
> have everything, and, if that be absent, all
> our actions are directed towards attaining it."

94. Everything is either a great idea, or a great story. To turn more ideas into action, try not to put off anything that can be done in under one minute, and try to nurture working and living environments that positively influences how you act and feel.

While some people are more sensitive to environmental influences than others, we are all affected by the conditions of the environments in which we spend large amounts of time. Cluttered environments are extremely effective at raising stress levels as our minds are over-stimulated by an onslaught of thought triggers. An overflowing "To be sorted" paperwork, unfinished projects, and unknown boxes of "Let's just keep this just in case" stuff, can all increase subconscious stress levels.

Here's some things you can do to allow the outer peace and order to permeate to inner peace and calm:

1. **Don't start with organising things into places.** Half of it probably doesn't need to be organised, it probably needs to be binned. Instead, start with *sorting out* the useful from the unneeded, and trash the rest. The first step is to get rid of stuff.
2. **Never label anything as miscellaneous**
3. **Don't accept freebies or bargains** if you don't need them. Question whether you can afford to accept the storage costs of additional water bottles, pens, or unneeded life accessories.
4. **Abandon dead projects.** Even with the best intentions in the world, there are some things that we're just not going to have the time to finish. The more unfinished things surround us, the more reminders we have of the things that failed. Be honest with yourself: accept, abandon, clear the space, clear your conscience, and move forward.
5. **Can you digitise it?** A digital photo of the things you are binning, keeps a permanent record without taking the space and can reduce the emotional burden of permanent separation.

95. We learn through experiences. Fear of commitment or postponing action with extended procrastination only holds us back from the greatest learning opportunity – *experience.* We too often allow fear to restrict ourselves from gaining that better viewpoint that is waiting for us from the next step.

    We would never wait for every traffic light to turn red before embarking on a journey like commuting to work, we make a start and improvise the journey as it unfolds. This approach usually works out better than waiting forever for impossibly perfect conditions. Committing to a direction unlocks the answers we simply cannot find from the starting point.

Some actions might involve some risk, and many actions may not turn out as expected, but the lessons we learn from experiences are priceless: new information enables better-informed decisions. We can then be grateful for the increased knowledge, grateful for the progress, grateful for the opportunity to progress along a journey worth taking.

Where might the next steps take you?

96. In 2005, Sonja Lyubomirsky of the University of California reported that in modern western society, there are three major factors contributing to a person's chronic happiness level[28]. This happiness level is a like our individual baseline of happiness which we return to after periods of temporary excitement or upset.

Circumstantial Effects have a surprisingly small impact on our long-term capacity to lead a happy life, primarily comprising one's spirituality and friendships, and also including factors such as health, wealth and perceived freedoms.

A far more significant factor influencing our baseline happiness is predetermined by our genes, noted as an individual's **Genetic Set Range**. This can be likened to our genetic disposition for weight.

Voluntary Control Factors make up the rest, including our ability to change one's natural thought habits through behavioural choices and attitudes.

Although our genetic makeup can shift as we grow up via activating epigenomes[29], the low availability of gene therapy today rules out the Genetic Set Range as a rational area of focus.

Our Circumstantial Effects only account for around 10% of the influence on our baseline happiness and are also often beyond our ability to influence. We can easily fall into the trap of looking for happiness only in these fragile and relatively insignificant external circumstances. It is great news therefore that over 40% of the potential influence of our baseline happiness is within our *Voluntary Control*.

Taking the steps in this book and enjoying both a genuinely improved life satisfaction and healthier emotional well-being, are within your voluntary control.

97. Here is a quick idea to help keep an eye on the target. To remember what really matters to you, personally you, specifically you, where you would like to be or how you would like to feel now and in the future.

Whatever it is that you are doing right there, right now, is taking you somewhere. As time continues to pass, so we continue to create a trail directed by our every decision. What we do in every moment, takes us somewhere, so keep in mind why you are doing that specific task, be aware of how it feels, and if it is progressing your life in a meaningful way.

If we only get one shot at life, where will you aim your shot? What target do you align your actions and decisions toward? They say if we aim for the moon, even if we miss we land among the stars.

98. Can you think of one small habit that you have, that is within your power to change? Write it down somewhere. Can you then write down another equally small habit that you would like to adopt? Maybe these could be something like: "Spending less time on social media", and "Have better posture" or "Be more patient" or "Make time to be creative". Look at both of these notes. Then, stick this second note directly in the way of somewhere you look so frequently that the desired habit pierces the conscious mind and bounces around all week! The centre of the bathroom mirror often works well.

If there is a location where you perform the unwanted habit most frequently, put the first note there. If the undesired habit is digitally based, could setting it as you desktop or smartphone background help? Or putting the social media apps into a folder and renaming it?

Next, can you remove the trigger? Is there something that triggers the bad habit that can be switched off, or removed? Can you find a trigger for the positive habit?

Habit forming takes effort and repetition, so you'll need to consciously try to make the change. Try to keep in mind why you are doing it – pruning your habits to maximise your happiness, ensures that you inevitably succeed!

99. Too often, it is only as we feel like we are parting ways with someone, that we find the courage to share our precious feelings of love and compassion. Too often, we reserve the sentiments of gratitude and appreciation, until these parting moments spur us on to face the vulnerability of sharing intimate emotions. "Thank you so much for the time we shared" or "I really appreciate you as a friend" or "Take care, I'll miss you" and of course "I love you".

When we share such deep feelings, be they of gratitude, of love, or of some other profound honesty, we allow ourselves to be open to much deeper and more meaningful connections. We remember that our lives are a meaningful part of something bigger.

At those magical vulnerable moments, we are finally true to our deepest emotions and find the courage to share them before the opportunity is lost. We don't have to save those vulnerable truths for those moments of impending separation. We are allowed to express positive emotions before the end of the phone call, before we say goodbye.

So instead of safeguarding an "I love you", or conserving a compliment until it bursts out at a goodbye, try to find the strength and courage to be honest without the motivation of a parting moment. We too often don't get a final goodbye and so much sadness can come from our unsaid words. Furthermore, so much potential happiness is lost from those same unsaid sentiments. So try being open and vulnerable without being spurred on by the threat of imminent separation. Motivate an honest conversation with love. Some things aren't worth waiting for.

Challenge yourself to write down five names, right now, that you will contact within the next week, and share with them a sincere, heartfelt sentiment, that you may have inadvertently been safeguarding.

You are making the world a better place.

100. Never miss a puddle on your journey. It is those times we get stuck in the mud that we learn things. It is those detours that make life interesting. It is falling off your bike just to get back on it, learning that to keep moving is the only way to keep our balance. It is taking the time to jump right in and get messy, because that, is where we truly come alive. Right in the thick of it, truly living, truly immersed, we experience "flow". It is taking enough time to experience every part of the journey while it is here and if we get a little wet and muddy along the way, we'll have had a smile on our faces to remind us what it's all about. So when you see a puddle, go be a kid, have fun, have joy, let go and feel alive, and when you get stuck in the mud know that you'll get yourself out, get back on your feet, back on the path, and be stronger on the other side of it ready for the next puddle to jump into...

Never miss a puddle on your journey.

THE COMPLETE MAP

Over the last 100 steps, we learned about the importance of increased happiness, and the types of things that influence how happy we feel, typically relating to either a person's mindset or elements of their lifestyle. Within the mindset part, we saw how pivotal one's perspective can be, how fundamentally imperative gratitude is, and how we can maximise this happiness-generating gratitude by training the mind to become as mindfully aware as possible while nurturing more frequent and dominant positive thoughts. Then, within the lifestyle part, we saw that some factors are internal to ourselves, while others provide a sense of connectedness and meaning within something greater than one human life. The mindset steps create a happier life, the happier life facilitates a happy mind.

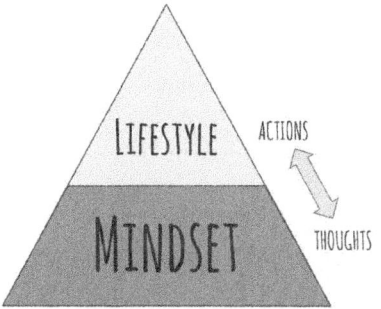

From here we became more familiar with the steps we can take in each area, and how only through taking action can we bring all the pieces together to create something of great power. This fully assembled environment for balanced sustainable happiness is shown on the next page:

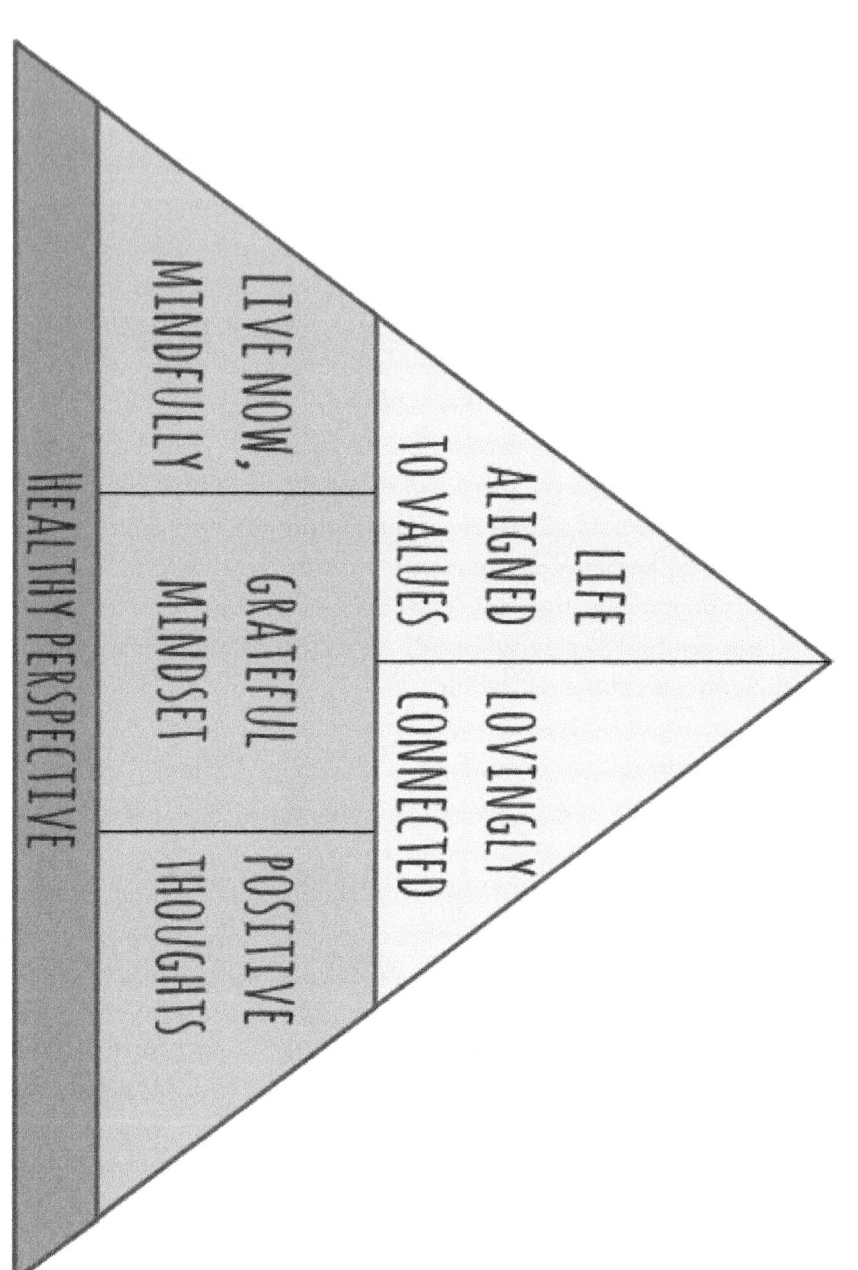

A STEP, A LEAP, A BOUND

So we are kitted out with our newly completed map of the happiness-increasing environment and we've got a handy guidebook of 100 steps we can take to progress our skills in each of the elements. But why just walk down the path step by step when we can leap toward ever-growing happiness in great bounds?

It is no challenge to admire the details of a map while staying firmly within the security of a comfort zone. It is even possible to grasp some general understanding of the terrain, to see where the paths lead and intersect, and some obstacles among the complexity of the land. It is something quite different to step out of the comfort of the known and bravely wander into those lands to begin enjoying the treasures it can only share through experience. Reading a menu never satiated an appetite; reading a prescription never cured an ailment.

To a complete beginner, it can seem near impossible to learn a musical instrument, let alone master one. Similarly, others may find it challenging to imagine being EVEN happier than they are right now. But the science proves otherwise. We openly accept we cannot play the violin without practice, and freely admit we can't run a marathon without training, but when it comes to learning how to live a happy life, we suddenly already know what is best for us. An unknown path cannot be seen until it is walked upon. But with practice, incremental results are inevitable. It is the law of nature, cause and effect. We can learn new languages, we adapt to new environments, we oftentimes change our physical habits, and we change our mental habits too. Like physical health, they can fluctuate and drift naturally, or they can be trained.

No guidebook can detail every intricacy of an individual's journey; only empower the reader to develop the skills and attitude to keep progressing autonomously. As Benjamin Disraeli said, "*Action may not always bring happiness; but there is no happiness without action.*"

Therefore this final step is for you to take real action. To challenge yourself and see the wonders a curious mind can achieve. This final step is for you to set resolutions with clear commitments, to challenge your comfort zone to turn small steps, into giant leaps.

Starting today, you are invited to challenge yourself with your own personal resolutions to develop happier habits. You can download a free Resolution Chart from www.AGoodWayToThink.com/Happiness-Archives.

As well as the 100 Steps in this book to inspire your resolutions, here's just a few more ideas that aim to get you out of the comfort zone and into the realm of real action and real results. The place the magic happens.

Donate Something – Someone else may need it more than you. Think of charity shops or those less materially well of and consider what you can give. Disused electronics? Neglected clothes? Other household goods? The fewer things we have the lighter we typically feel. Can you donate something every day for a week?

Pay it Forwards! Could you pay for the next person's coffee, or buy an extra parking ticket and leave it in the machine?

Meditate – can you take 10 minutes every day for a week to stop the rushing around and check in with yourself? Check in on the body, and the mind, how are you feeling. It may be just 10 – 15 minutes each day, but it brings such benefits to so many people. Give it fair trial and see how it works for you. Head over to the free articles section of AGoodWayToThink.com for a handy explanation of meditation for beginners and other mind cleaning techniques.

Greet People Warmly – From passers-by in the street to people you see almost every day, step up your greetings for a week with genuine Hello's, friendly eyes, and big smiles.

Speak to Someone Lonely – Everyone likes to be asked if they're alright, can you visit a friend or relative or just make a phone call. You may be surprised what you see when your eyes are opened wider, and surprised what you can give when your heart is.

Be Anonymously Kind – Can you do these challenges without any desire for recognition? Donate without expecting remuneration, pay it forwards with solely compassion, meditate without bragging, greet people just so they feel special, talk to someone purely for their benefit. Just look what happens when you are anonymously kind.

Well, here we are at the end of this little guidebook. Perhaps it will be a map to ease you through simple, exciting changes on your journey of ever-increasing happiness; or perhaps it will nestle among your subconscious thoughts waiting for a time of greater motivation in future. If something on these pages has planted a seed of an idea or awoken an understanding already within you, have the confidence to allow it to grow by investing some time in it, water it with thought, nourish it with energy and patience, such that it stands a chance of flourishing in your soul. Give them fair trial. If there are things that don't work for you or that you would like to change or personalise, go ahead. There is no mandate or doctrine for happiness, just some tried and tested research., but we all walk in our own unique ways.

If the guidebook has fulfilled its purpose with you, why not pass it on to someone else that likes being happy? Who knows where it will continue on its happiness sharing journey, as you continue on yours.

If you would like to continue taking steps to ever-greater happiness, search for A Good Way To Think and join the community. We run one-to-one sessions online, deliver group happiness training courses, and continue to share the latest life-enhancing exercises in applied happiness every week.

Personally, I would like to thank you sincerely for whatever you do to help make the world an *even happier* place.

Your actions truly change the world!

References

1. Step 9: *Pursuing Happiness in Everyday Life: The Characteristics and Behaviors of Online Happiness Seekers.* Acacia C. Parks, Matthew D. Della Porta, Russell S. Pierce, Ran Zilca, and Sonja Lyubomirsky. Online First Publication, May 28, 2012. DOI: 10.1037/a0028587

2. Guy after Step 21 & Step 94: The Benefits of Frequent Positive Affect: Does Happiness Lead to Success? Lyubomirsky, Sonja; King, Laura; Diener, E. Psychological Bulletin, Vol 131(6), Nov 2005, 803-855. DOI: 10.1037/0033-2909.13.6.803

3. Step 22: *The human emotional brain without sleep: A prefrontal-amygdala disconnect* Yoo SS, Gujar N, Hu P, Jolesz FA & Walker MP. Current Biology 2007; 17(20): 877-878

4. Steps 38 & 47: *Mindfulness-based stress reduction for older adults: effects on executive function, frontal alpha asymmetry and immune function.* Moynihan JA1, Chapman BP, Klorman R, Krasner MS, Duberstein PR, Brown KW, Talbot NL. 2013;68(1):34-43. DOI: 10.1159/000350949. Epub 2013 Jun 15

5. Guy after Step 48: Feeling Good about Giving: The Benefits (and Costs) of Self-Interested Charitable Behavior. Anik, Lalin and Aknin, Lara B. and Norton, Michael I. and Dunn, Elizabeth W., Feeling Good About Giving: The Benefits (and Costs) of Self-Interested Charitable Behavior (August 6, 2009). Harvard Business School.

6. Step 60: *Is Psychological Well-being Linked to the Consumption of Fruit and Vegetables?* David G. Blanchflower – Dartmouth College, Andrew J. Oswald – University of Warwick,

Sarah Stewart-Brown – University of Warwick Medical School UK. DOI: 10.3386/w18469

7.   Step 60: *On carrots and curiosity: eating fruit and vegetables is associated with greater flourishing in daily life.* T S Conner, K L Brookie, A C Richardson, M A Polak. Br J Health Psychol. 2015 May;20(2):413-27. DOI: 10.1111/bjhp.12113

8.   Step 60: *Many apples a day keep the blues away--daily experiences of negative and positive affect and food consumption in young adults.* B A White, C C Horwath, T S Conner – University of Otago. Br J Health Psychol. 2013 Nov;18(4):782-98. DOI: 10.1111/bjhp.12021

9.   Step 61: *UVA Irradiation of Human Skin Vasodilates Arterial Vasculature and Lowers Blood Pressure Independently of Nitric Oxide Synthase.* Martin Feelisch - University of Southampton, Richard B. Weller - University of Edinburgh, et al. Journal of Investigative Dermatology (2014) 134, 1839-1846; DOI: 10.1038/jid.2014.27

10.   Step 64: *Identification of an immune-responsive mesolimbocortical serotonergic system: Potential role in regulation of emotional behavior.* Lowry CA, et al. Neuroscience (2007), doi: 10.1016/j.neuroscience.2007.01.067

11.   Step 64: *Can bacteria make you smarter?.* American Society for Microbiology, May 25, 2010

12.   Step 70: *The effect of acute aerobic exercise on positive activated affect: A meta-analysis. Psychology of Sport and Exercise.* J. Reed and D.S. Ones, 2006, 7(5), 477-514. DOI: :10.1016/j.psychsport.2005.11.003

13.   Step 70: *Effects of Physical Exercise on Depressive Symptoms and Biomarkers in Depression.* Archer T. – University of Gothenburg, Josefsson T. – Halmstad University, Lindwall M. – University of Gothenburg. Pubmed ID: 25470398

14.   Step 77: *The health consequences of hostility, Anger and hostility in cardiovascular and behavioral disorders* W. Barefoot et al., Margaret A. Chesney and Ray H. Rosenman. Hemisphere Publishing Corp., 1985. DOI: 10.1002/smi.2460030220

15.   Step 79: *Dynamic spread of happiness in a large social network: longitudinal analysis over 20 years in the Framingham Heart Study.* BMJ 2008;337:a2338. DOI:10.1136/bmj.a2338

16.   Step 79: *The Dynamics of Personal Influence.* Nicholas A. Christakis. See also *The Collective Dynamics of Smoking in a Large Social Network* N Engl J Med 2008; 358:2249-2258, May 22, 2008 DOI: 10.1056/NEJMsa0706154

17.   Step 85 *Spontaneous trait transference: communicators take on the qualities they describe in others* Skowronski JJ - Ohio State University et al. DOI: 10.1037/0022-3514.74.4.837

18.   Step 86: *Mirrored Emotion* Lydialyle Gibson. The University of Chicago Magazine, April 2006, Vol. 98, Issue 4

19.   Step 93: *Longevity Increased by Positive Self-Perceptions of Aging* Becca R. Levy and Martin D. Slade - Yale University, et al. Journal of Personality and Social Psychology, 2002, Vol. 83, No. 2, 261-270 DOI: 10.1037//0022-3514.83.2.261

20.   Guy after 54 and Step 93: *The heart's content: The association between positive psychological well-being and cardiovascular health.* Boehm, Julia K.; Kubzansky, Laura D. -

Harvard University. Psychological Bulletin, Vol 138(4), Jul 2012, 655-691. DOI: 10.1037/a0027448

21. Steps 94: *Initial results from a study of the effects of meditation on multitasking performance* David M. Levy — University of Washington, DOI: 10.1145/19797421979862

22. Step 94: *Mindfulness meditation improves cognition: Evidence of brief mental training* Fadel Zeidan — Wake Forest University School of Medicine, DOI: 10.1016/j.concog.2010.03.014

23. Step 94: *Enhancing Compassion: A Randomized Controlled Trial of a Compassion Cultivation Training Program* Hooria Jazaier. DOI 10.1007/s10902-012-9373-z

24. Step 94: *Compassion Training Alters Altruism and Neural Responses to Suffering* Weng HY, Fox AS, Shackman AJ, Stodola DE, Caldwell JZK, Olson MC, et al. University of Wisconsin. Psychological Science May 21, 2013 DOI: 10.1177/0956797612469537

25. Step 94: *Open hearts build lives: Positive emotions, induced through loving-kindness meditation, build consequential personal resources.* Fredrickson, Barbara L.; Cohn, Michael A.; Coffey, Kimberly A.; Pek, Jolynn; Finkel, Sandra M. Journal of Personality and Social Psychology, Vol 95(5), Nov 2008, 1045-1062. DOI: 10.1037/a0013262

26. Step 94: *Alterations in Brain and Immune Function Produced by Mindfulness Meditation* Davidson, Richard J. PhD; Kabat-Zinn, Jon PhD et al. DOI: 10.1097/01.PSY.0000077505.67574.E3

27. Step 94: *Effect of compassion meditation on neuroendocrine, innate immune and behavioral responses to*

psychosocial stress Thaddeus W.W. Pace et al. Emory University School of Medicine August 2008. DOI: 10.1016/j.psyneuen.2008.08.011

28. Step 97: *Pursuing Happiness: The Architecture of Sustainable Change.* Sonja Lyubomirsky , Kennon M. Sheldon , David Schkade. DOI: 10.1037/1089-2680.9.2.111

29. Step 97: *Epigenetic differences arise during the lifetime of monozygotic twins.* Mario F. Fraga et al. DOI: 10.1073/pnas.0500398102

The word "Happy" comes from the Icelandic word Happ, meaning luck or chance, though we now use the word to describe something far more complex than an uncontrollable stroke of luck. The next time you're feeling happy, take a minute to consider just how lucky humanity is to have the capacity to feel such an enjoyable state. Happiness transcends luck. It transcends chance. We can choose to influence our happiness for the better! It is within our voluntary control.
Don't forget to make your life memorable!

Glossary

Adrenaline — A stress-response hormone also called epinephrine, secreted by the medulla of the adrenal gland, and is a crucial part of the body's fight, flight or freeze response by causing air passages to dilate and the heart to beat faster to provide the muscles with extra oxygen, while redirecting additional blood to the major muscle groups. Over exposure can be damaging to health.

Amygdala — A part of the Limbic System in the brain important for emotional response, especially feelings of stress, fear and anger.

Cortisol — A stress hormone like adrenalin, activated by the fight, flight, freeze response. Moderate levels can help provide motivation for action, however, higher levels of these stress hormones reduce serotonin levels and accelerate the ageing process of DNA replication

Dopamine — The neurotransmitter that underlies motivation, helps control the pleasure and reward centres of the brain, and promotes engagement by adding a zest for life.

Endorphins — A family of morphine based chemicals produced within the body, ie. endogenous morphines. Often responsible for feelings of elation and euphoria after intense exercise.

Equanimity – A balanced mindset developed through much practice, where one learns to observe the present moment without getting carried away with desires, wishes, hopes and cravings for a certain outcome or specific situation to happen. Similarly, it includes learning to avoid emotional repulsion or aversion to undesired outcomes or situations. Simply observing the nature of the reality of the present moment, without emotional labelling. This is a highly valued skill in the Buddhist community, as learning how to truly face the present moment with equanimity, allows the mind to be free from all unhappiness, all suffering, and enjoy real peace, real harmony.

Executive Functions – Conscious mental activities directed by the prefrontal cortex in the brain, including short-term memory, information processing, attention regulation, decision-making, emotional regulation, prioritising inhibition and self-awareness.

Happiness Intelligence – A not-yet-standardised quotient used by A Good Way To Think, similar to IQ and EQ, relating to a person's proficiency of applying the skills and techniques that result in sustainable happiness.

Joy – Not to be mistaken for Happiness, joy is not dependent on longer term meaning and is only the present moment experience of serotonin, such as delight and ecstasy. Joy sustains none of longer term elements of true happiness, such as those in part two of this book.

Melatonin – A hormone that helps regulate appetite and sleep patterns, produced by the pineal gland in the brain.

When it's dark, the pineal gland produces melatonin to make you feel sleepy.

Mindfulness

> Informal Mindfulness Living – Mindfulness means paying attention, on purpose and non-judgmentally, to the present moment. It is the practice of observing your body and mind, thoughts and feelings, as though from a distance, without any attachment, or trying to suppress or deny them.
>
> Formal Mindfulness Meditation – Being still for a moment to observe the breath or the thoughts or the information from the sense doors that exist in this present moment. When concentration inevitably drifts to the future or past, patiently, keep bringing the attention back to the sensations of the present moment.

Neural Darwinism – The naturally occurring process within the brain pruning less used synapses, redirecting blood flow and enhancing synapses in those more active areas of the brain.

Neuroplasticity – The recurring changes in the neural pathways of the brain caused by changes in environment or behaviour, thought habits and emotions.

NLP / Neuro-Linguistic Programming – an approach to communication looking at the connections between neurological processes, language, and behavioural patterns, and how one can be altered to influence another.

Oxytocin – Nicknamed "the love hormone", is responsible for feelings of emotional connection, such as our relationships with others and a sense of connectedness. It is released during physical contact, and spikes during childbirth, breastfeeding and during intimate contact and orgasm.

Positive Affect – The extent to which an individual subjectively experiences positive moods such as joy, interest, enthusiasm, contentedness and alertness.

Sense Doors – The six parts of the body responsible for a certain type of sensory inputs signals received by the brain. Those being the eyes, the ears, the sensory nervous system, the nose, tongue, and mind.

Serotonin – A hormone that affects mood, appetite and sleep, it is arguably the most important biological chemical within our happiness systems. It is also a neurotransmitter, meaning that it transmits messages between nerve cells within the nervous system and brain.

This copy has been read by:

This book has travelled to:

#0220 - 080517 - C0 - 210/148/7 - PB - DID1835394